VI KIPLING FSNU

MYTHS AND

MISCONCEPTIONS

OF

SPIRITUALISM

by

Vi Kipling FSNU

Published in 2010

by

SDU PUBLICATIONS
www.s-upton.com

for

The Spiritualists' National Union

ISBN 9781905961214

Copyright © SNU 2010
www.snu.org.uk

Printed and bound in Great Britain by
CPI Antony Rowe, Chippenham and Eastbourne

PT6

TABLE OF CONTENTS

INTRODUCTION

This book originally started life as a Thesis which was printed as a small booklet. It was written in order to show that some of the myths and misconceptions contained within Spiritualism, or thought to be part of Spiritualism, are so illogical it is difficult to understand why some people believe in, and others pay lip service to, them.

It is accepted that people will always have their own beliefs and many appear to draw comfort from holding opinions and views on matters which I consider to be sheer nonsense and it is, consequently, an unfortunate fact that I may very well tread on many pet corns. I must, therefore, right from the outset, state quite categorically that the opinions I hold, are based on my own researches and experiences with both spirit discarnate and spirit incarnate stretching over more than 40 years and are not intended to be critical of other people's opinions or experiences.

It was Silver Birch, the spirit guide of Maurice Barbanell, whom the majority of Spiritualists and Mediums hold in very high esteem, who said: "If your reason cannot accept it, then reject it." I have rejected much upon my spiritual pathway, not necessarily because at that point I had insufficient knowledge to understand it, but mainly because there was insufficient evidence to support the claim(s) made. I have also readjusted my thinking time and again along this pathway as new evidence and experiences have been gained. Perhaps some of the contents of this book may cause some people to re-evaluate their thinking.

Each section will be devoted to what I see as a Myth, or Misconception; how it is envisioned or understood by many, followed by my reasons for my refusal to accept it. It is hoped that the reasons outlined will be given serious consideration and not rejected out of hand. There is so much we will never understand about the world of spirit until we are actually inhabiting it; even the spirit guides contradict each other on various matters so it can be difficult to establish facts regarding some subjects.

For ease of reference the sections have been put into alphabetical order under two main headings of 'What is not Spiritualism' and 'What is not Spirit'. The final section 'This is Spiritualism' is dedicated to Maurice Barbanell who wrote a book with this title and was the first book I read which explained Spiritualism so simply for me and to whom I will always be grateful.

All the matters discussed in the various sections have been thought by many people to be part of the Science, Philosophy and Religion of Spiritualism. I am sure that most of you, at one time or another, have had to spend a lot of time explaining to people that some of the things they talk about and which are high-lighted in this book, have no place in Spiritualism. Spiritualism is a religion and not part of the Occult. One of the dictionary definitions of the word occult is "That which is unknown" into which category Spiritualism certainly does not fall.

Some readers of this book may be very new to Spiritualism so if I may, I would suggest that you use it as a Reference Book and if you find yourself in a discussion where the subject matter appears to be slightly 'fantastic', then please use this book to check its credibility. There are some facts surrounding Spiritualism and Mediumship which are well-known and some which are little known and because Spiritualism is not a subject which is taught in school; it does not appear to be in the religious curriculum, then perhaps students of Spiritualism, especially newcomers, can use this book to aid them in their search for understanding of spiritual matters.

On a personal level I find Spiritualism and spirit contact cluttered with a lot of unnecessary baggage and I am a little surprised, therefore, that we have so many people wishing to develop mediumship and consequently taking on this baggage. I really do think it is time to throw out the dirty bathwater while embracing the baby and keeping it safe.

July 2004
Vi receives the Fellowship of the SNU from
Vice-President, Minister Dinah Annable

3

WHAT IS NOT SPIRITUALISM

ALIENS

Have we been visited by beings from other planets? Are there other life forms in our galaxy – in other galaxies in other universes and do they have the technology to visit Earth? All things are possible. These beings may or may not speak our language. I would think, however, that if they have the technology and scientific acumen to visit Earth from far distant reaches of the universe, then learning English would not be too big a problem to them. It is possible, however, as many seem to think, that as mediums communicate between two worlds (the physical world and the spirit world) by means of telepathy, then it would make sense for aliens to communicate with Earth using the receptive telepathic skills of mediums.

Mediums have learned, through development and training, to expand their awareness and open up the channel of communication using the energy of thought. This is how mental mediumship works - by telepathy between the two worlds of existence - physical and spirit.

So it is feasible for a medium to claim that they have been contacted and have communicated with extra-terrestrials. Most mediums, however, do know that one of the responsibilities of mediumship is to give evidence of survival and to claim communication with extra-terrestrials would need a lot of evidence before the world, or other mediums, will take them seriously.

Since approximately 1990 the word 'channelling' has crept into the Spiritualist vocabulary and usually indicates that the medium has entered a state of entrancement and words have been spoken through him or her, by people not of this world. In the main it has been people from the spirit world but it has been known for the medium to claim that they are being entranced to allow an alien to speak to our world. It has not been satisfactorily established whether the alien controlling the medium is alive (in his/her/its physical body) and exerting the control from a spaceship or the planet on which this being lives or, whether it is the spirit of an alien which used to live on the named planet.

Reading the transcripts of some of these alien utterances leaves me of the opinion that I could, in fact, be reading words given by spirit, so similar are they, in some cases. In others, then I am afraid I hesitate to wonder where the information is coming from and solid evidence would have to be given for it to be acceptable.

If aliens are contacting us, through mediums and/or other people, and I concede that this can happen, then why aren't they giving the world and its leaders some definite evidence of who they are, where they live, an indication of their superior technology (as much as we can understand of course) so that some kind of evidence can be gleaned to support their claims of who they are and where they originate from.

Perhaps this has already been tried and was not successful because the claims were laughed at by the people approached. If this is the case then different people should be approached. The scientists are not as closed-minded as many people think and do, like any intelligent person will, allow that there could very well be life forms on other planets and that it would be very egotistical of us to think that the whole of this universes, and all the others yet to be discovered, were created just for Man.

If there are aliens trying to communicate through mediums then a different approach has to be found as at the moment any talking they are doing has no substance or substantiation. This really makes me feel that a race(s) which would have to be highly intelligent and technically advanced to try and contact us would, therefore, have the ability to do so, without having to use mediums who have no political power and belong to a religion that has spent practically the whole of its life fighting the image being laid upon it by others.

The mediums communicating with aliens may not be Spiritualists, they may be working as independent mediums but as soon as the word 'medium' is heard, then the power of association relates it across to 'Spiritualism'. For some people the world 'Spiritualism' itself is associated with aliens, demons, hobgoblins and things that go bump in the night so let's not feed their ignorance

Mediums making claims that they are being visited by aliens should enjoy such visits but keep it private until they are able to support these claims with firm evidence. I am surprised that any medium would make such a claim without first establishing the facts as most mediums are trained to give evidence and it is usually the first thing they look for.

Spiritualism is a Religion, a Science and a Philosophy; it is not a springboard for aliens and while a claim for investigating aliens within the séance room could be fit into the Science of Spiritualism, aliens are not part of the Religion or Philosophy of Spiritualism. The Religion of Spiritualism will accept the possibility of aliens but the Philosophy of Spiritualism is founded on facts and until there are sufficient facts available to support the claims of alien visitors then there is no place in Spiritualism for aliens.

And . . . . one final thought . . . .

Unless they are spirit aliens, they really wouldn't come under the umbrella of Spiritualism, with or without evidence.

ALTERNATE THERAPIES

CRYSTAL HEALING

"Crystal healing has been used for thousands of years. Crystals heal holistically. They work on our emotional, physical, mental and spiritual levels of being.

Our bodies are made up of whirling vortexes of energy known as Chakras which are located within our spine. These whirling vortexes of energy extend from the spine out the front of our bodies. When a chakra is out of balance or becomes blocked our body's natural flow of energy is disrupted causing symptoms such as pain, fatigue, listlessness, stress and depression to name a few.

Crystals work through vibration. When used, crystals re-align the Chakras located within our bodies which in turn re-balances the bio magnetic sheath that surrounds and inter-penetrates our physical body. By placing crystals on the affected Chakras any blockages in these whirling vortexes of energy can be cleared away allowing our body's energies to flow freely again.

Because of the way crystals vibrate and the individual healing properties they hold, crystals heal holistically. That is to say that they can heal on all levels i.e. our subtle bodies (aura) and our physical body. This can be achieved by just holding the crystal, putting it under our pillow at night, leaving it by our bedside table, carrying it about on *crystal* our person or by placing it on certain parts of the body. *(Jewelle)*

It is possible to heighten the effect of the crystal's energy when healing others with crystals. By working with your own body's healing abilities it is possible to focus healing energies and channel it through the crystal. This amplifies the healing properties of the crystal helping to cleanse the client's body of any negativity or clear any blockages of their chakras.

Crystal healing can help with all sorts of problems whether they be emotional or physical. By placing crystals on blocked chakras they can help alleviate symptomatic problems such as headaches, tiredness, depression, pain and so on, the list is endless. Crystals are also very effective for emotional stress, helping to lift negativity and get rid of that 'heavy' feeling. Lots of people come across the feeling of 'heaviness' during their working day but do not recognise the significance of the fact that we all collect negativity and if this is not off loaded it will affect how we function. Crystals can clear negativity allowing our bodies energy centres to function as they should.

A crystal healing session usually lasts for 1 hour during which the recipient is fully clothed."[1]

REIKI HEALING (palm-Healy)

"Reiki is a spiritual developed in 1922 by Mikao Usui. After three weeks of fasting and meditating on Mount Kurama, in Japan, Usui claimed to receive the ability of "healing without energy depletion". A portion of the practice, tenohira or palm healing, is used as a form of complementary and alternative medicine (CAM). Tenohira is a technique whereby practitioners believe they are moving "healing energy" (a form of ki) through the palms.

Neither the existence of ki nor any mechanism for its manipulation are scientifically proven, and a systematic review of randomized clinical trials conducted in 2008 did not support the efficacy of reiki or its recommendation for use in the treatment of any condition.

WHOLE BODY TREATMENT

In a typical whole-body Reiki treatment, the practitioner asks the recipient to lie down, usually on a

---

[1] www.crystalhealing.org.uk

massage table, and relax. Loose, comfortable clothing is usually worn during the treatment. The practitioner might take a few moments to enter a calm or meditative state of mind and mentally prepare for the treatment, that is usually carried out without any unnecessary talking.

The treatment proceeds with the practitioner placing his hands on the recipient in various positions. However, practitioners may use a non-touching technique, where the hands are held a few centimetres away from the recipient's body, for some or all of the positions. The hands are usually kept still for 3 to 5 minutes before moving to the next position. Overall, the hand positions usually give a general coverage of the head, the front and back of the torso, the knees and feet. Between 12 and 20 positions are used, with the whole treatment lasting 45 to 90 minutes.

Some practitioners use a fixed set of hand positions. Others use their intuition to guide them as to where treatment is needed, sometimes starting the treatment with a "scan" of the recipient to find such areas. The intuitive approach might also lead to individual positions being treated for much shorter or longer periods of time.

It is reported that the recipient often feels warmth or tingling in the area being treated, even when a non-touching approach is being used. A state of deep relaxation, combined with a general feeling of well-being, is usually the most noticeable immediate effect of the treatment, although emotional releases can also occur. As the Reiki treatment is said to be stimulating natural healing processes, instantaneous "cures" of specific health problems are not usually observed. A series of three or more treatments, typically at intervals of 1 to 7 days, is usually recommended if a chronic condition is being addressed. Regular treatments, on an on-going basis, can be used with the aim of maintaining well-being. The interval between such treatments is typically in the range of 1 to 4 weeks, except in the case of *self-treatment* when a daily practice is common."[1]

REFLEXOLOGY

"Reflexology, or zone therapy, is the practice of massaging, squeezing, or pushing on parts of the feet, or sometimes the hands and ears, with the goal of encouraging a beneficial effect on other parts of the body, or to improve general health.

The precursor of modern reflexology was introduced to the United States in 1913 by William H Fitzgerald, MD (1872-1942), an ear, nose, and throat specialist, and Dr. Edwin Bowers. Fitzgerald claimed that applying pressure had an aesthetic effect on other areas of the body.

Reflexology was further developed in the 1930s and 1940s by Eunice D. Ingham (1899-1974), a nurse and physiotherapist. Ingham claimed that the feet and hands were especially sensitive, and mapped the entire body into "reflexes" on the feet. It was at this time that "zone therapy" was renamed reflexology.

Modern reflexologists in the United States and the United Kingdom often learn Ingham's method first, although there are other more recently developed methods.

There is no consensus on how reflexology is supposed to work; a unifying theme is the idea that areas on the foot correspond to areas of the body, and that by manipulating these one can improve health through one's qi.

Concerns have been raised by medical professionals that treating potentially serious illnesses with reflexology, which has no proven efficacy, could

---

[1] www.wikipedia.com

delay the seeking of help from proven conventional medicine. There is no clinical or scientific evidence that reflexology has any beneficial effect"[1]

These are only three therapies out of many which are thought to be part of Spiritualism. For some people, they are introduced to these therapies within a Spiritualist Church. A demonstration of the therapy is given by an experienced practitioner and because it was first experienced in a Spiritualist Church, it remains in the mind of some as part of the practices of Spiritualism.

The only therapy which is part of the religion of Spiritualism is Spirit Healing and this isn't in fact, an alternative therapy - it is a complementary therapy in that Spirit Healing does not replace orthodox medicine, it works with it and complements it.

SPIRIT HEALING ✶✶ (Course)

"'Spiritual Healing' and 'healing' mean a form of healing by the use of forces and energies from the world of spirit channelled through the healer by the laying on of hands on or near the body, or prayer or the direction of thought from a distance."[2]

Spirit Healing must never be confused with any of the alternative therapies which are available and it is only Spirit Healing which is found within Spiritualist Churches. It is accepted that many Spiritualists are practitioners of some of these other therapies with excellent qualifications in those fields but they must ensure that they don't inadvertently give the impression that their abilities within these specific areas are part of Spiritualism.

---

[1] www.wikipedia.com
[2] Spiritualists' National Union's Bye-Laws H, Part I, 2(a)

ANGEL GUIDES

There seems to be a great deal of confusion regarding Spirit Guides and Angels with quite a lot of mediums claiming to have angels acting as Spirit Guides. While many may wish this could be true, there is no evidence whatsoever for such a supposition. When we look at it logically, we have to ask the question "Why would Angels do the job for which Spirit Guides are trained and at which they excel? There is no purpose served.

The philosophy of Spiritualism falls into the School of Realistic Philosophy as it is factually based. Spiritualists assert "There is no death; life continues and communication between the two worlds of being can, and does, take place." This assertion is then validated by the information contained in the spirit messages, given through the faculty of mediumship. Evidence of a communicating spirit's survival of death is given to the recipient of such a contact by a member of his/her spirit family and/or friends. It is communicators whose lives are known in great intimacy by their families that provide evidence for survival, not angels or even guides for that matter.

I think it is important at this stage that we look at the role of the Spirit Guides to try and establish why Angels would want to put them out of work.

A lot of the source material for this book is taken from the Silver Birch books and his answer to the question regarding "How the guides are selected?" is:

"Some volunteer because they are aware of tasks to be performed in your world. Others who have reached a maturity of spiritual growth are approached by those who have taken upon themselves the task of helping humanity.

"I was asked - I did not choose in the first place. But when I was asked whether I would volunteer to do so I readily assented and I can tell you that a very black picture was painted of the difficulties that would have to be surmounted before any progress could be made.

Yet those difficulties, to a large extent, have been conquered and the obstacles that still stand in the way are very small compared with those that have been removed."

"And those who volunteer, as distinct from those who are approached, do they have to satisfy some examiners who test their fitness to become guides?" was the next question.

"It is not quite in that sense," answered Silver Birch, "but something very like it. Our world is very highly organised, it is far more organised than ever you have thought was possible, and to perform this task requires a miniature organisation"

"Now you cannot get your group, your band, unless it is attracted to you for the work's sake and you have reached that degree of evolution which gives you the power of attraction. In our world what you are determines what you do. It is your spirit that is the dominant reality. There are no masks, no disguises, no subterfuges, no cheats; there is nothing hidden, all is known."

"And your fitness is apparent by what is seen in your spirit," was a sitter's comment.

"Yes, because your aura, your colours, your radiation, show what you are. None could masquerade as a teacher unless he was a teacher because it would be apparent he could not teach. And so you cannot attract the souls interested in the task of helping humanity unless you are ready to attract them by virtue of your own spiritual growth. Do you understand that?"

"Yes," the guide was told by the sitter asking these questions. "All I am trying to get at is how are spirits, who are not sufficiently evolved, prevented from acting as guides, although they may not have the same skill as one more evolved?"

"They just could not do it. You could not do that for which you are not fitted. You would not attract the power, the force, the rays, the people. You would have none of the accessories because you had not earned them. You could not control a medium without the help of those people. These are intricate processes."

"They appear simple when all is successful, but when things go wrong you get an inkling into the organisation behind apparently simple processes."[1]

It can be seen therefore, that each medium attracts to them the guides who are best suited to help them with the work they are to do.

Leading from Spirit Guides, in whom everyone is interested and wants one, we also have to establish the placement of Spirit Guardians who are more commonly known as Guardian Angels.

We are told by spirit teachers that there is some great soul in spirit allotted to each one of us at birth, or perhaps even before birth, who will remain with us throughout our earthly life; guiding where allowed but always there to support and comfort with the energy of their love. Some people confuse these souls with Spirit Guides whose role is to work with people who are developing their mediumship; Spirit Guardians remain with us no matter where our pathway in life may take us.

---

[1] Spirit Speaks

It appears that since the year 2,000 the earth has been over-run by angels; prior to 2,000 angels have always been acknowledged and are part of some religions but now angel culture has sprung up and they have been commercialised as never before, outside, of course, the religious confines.

People meet angels; have angelic visions; communicate with angels; receive signs from angels; channel angels; receive guidance from angels; run or organise angel workshops which are mainly very expensive to attend. In these workshops people are encouraged to accept that angels work with them as guides without any evidence for this whatsoever. It is a fact, however, that people do want to think that they walk with angels and these same celestial beings will protect them from life. While I do appreciate that some people are warned of avoidable accidents, we cannot expect to live our lives wrapped in a huge blanket of protection afforded by angels or spirit guides; there would be no point in living our lives on earth because basically we wouldn't be living them - we would be living our lives under a control and I am sure that is not the purpose of our earthly existence.

Spirit teachings, given when the mediums are in a state of deep trance, talk of Spirit Guides, never of Angels and it would be supposed that if Angels did take up the reins of guidance for certain individuals, there would be some record of this. I am sure there have been books written recently where it is claimed Angels are the communicating spirits but if this is the case then some form of substantiating evidence for this should be forthcoming.

Spirit Guides have proved their existence over and over again, not only through trance mediumship, but they have materialised in physical seances and spoken of themselves and their lives on earth to the sitters. There are many photographs taken at these seances showing the guides in all their splendour. There are no photographs of Angels manifesting in a materialised form so again, the question must be asked "Why not?"

Turning again to Silver Birch we find the following information about the guide:

WHO IS SILVER BIRCH (Spirit guide)

"Silver Birch is not my name. It is the name of the Indian spirit I use as a transformer that enables me to lower my vibrations and reach your world. The name does not matter. I have not revealed the name I bore on earth because it has no value so far as I am concerned.

I am not a Red Indian. I belong to another race in another part of the world that goes back much further.

We have what could be called a hierarchy. These are evolved spiritual beings - masters, if you like. Their task is to ensure the harmonious working of plans that have been made.

I was asked if I would forfeit what I have earned through evolution, and return as close as I could come to your world and act as a messenger for these evolved beings. My function would be to transmit their teachings so that those who were ready would be able to realise what we have to offer.

I agreed to do so, and that is the mission on which I have been engaged for a long time.

I had to learn your English language. It is not a language which I spoke when I was on earth. I was told when I embarked on my mission that I would have to familiarise myself with the language you use, its grammar and its syntax.

There was a problem, because I required a medium to make contact with your world. I could not reach it myself, because the stage of evolution I had reached was of a different vibration and not suitable for that purpose. I had to have what you call a transformer.

They found for me the spirit body of a Red Indian that was suitable to be my medium for transmitting the teachings which are given to me to impart.

I am not an infallible spirit teacher who never makes mistakes and has achieved the summit of progress. That cannot be so, because progress is eternal. There is no period to perfection, because the more you achieve the more you realise there is to be achieved.

The great value of what we have to offer is a sublime truth from the storehouse of divine wisdom and inspiration. We never ask you to take us on trust. We do not say that you must do what we suggest. Nor do we insist that there are no other ways by which you can obtain a greater attunement with the Great Spirit.

What we do affirm, and with all the strength at our command, is that the truths of the spirit can be tested by your reason, intelligence, and experience. There is no threat of punishment if you say we have told you things which you do not accept.

The Great Spirit has endowed you with a measure of free will. You are not puppets. You have intelligence, reason the ability to judge, to decide, to reflect, to form your own opinions and to be guided by the experiences that come your way.

It is only when the soul is in adversity that some of its greatest possibilities can be realised. You will not attain spiritual mastery in six easy lessons. It is a difficult path to tread. And as you tread it the familiar signposts and landmarks are left behind. But the more you progress, the more you achieve an inner confidence based on what you have earned for yourself.

Forget the past. It is behind you; what is in front of you is more important.

Naturally the past was responsible for the causes producing the effects which you are now experiencing, but you are producing the causes that in turn will produce the effects - try to sow the right seeds which is a platitude but still true. Have no fear; fear is the child of ignorance. Live in the light of knowledge."[1]

From the above, therefore, it must be obvious that an Angel, whose vibrations must be practically the quickest possible, could never appear as an Angel. This beautiful and highly evolved spiritual being would have to work on the same principles as Silver Birch and find people in the spirit realms to help him slacken his vibrations, or use their vibrations, in order for him to touch the vibrations of earth.

It is not intended to limit God, Angels, Spirit Guides or Guardians when it is said that Angels do not act as Guides as I am sure that if the need arose, this could, and would, take place. It is a known fact that there are many people, called mystics, who have had experiences of such a spiritual nature they enter a state of ecstatic bliss wherein they are 'at one with the ALL'. There are too many people, over the years, who have had these experiences to ignore them so all things can be possible but, perhaps, in special circumstances rather than the norm.

It is easy to understand, however, how a Spirit Guide could be mistaken for an Angel. If a Spirit Guide appears, in a spontaneous vision, to an inexperienced medium, there is often a radiance surrounding this soul

---

[1] Light from Silver Birch

accompanied by an emanation of deep peace. The recipient of such a vision really does feel that s/he is in the presence of someone wondrous - an Angel? No. A beautiful Spirit Guide with whom we are privileged and honoured to share time, and work with, for the spirit cause.

When a medium is entranced, even on a very light level, by one of his/her Spirit Guides, the influence of the Guide can be so powerful that the medium will be overcome by the sheer beauty of the personality which draws near. A feeling of deep love for all people and a compassion beyond that ever experienced before will also be felt, and quite often tears will pour from the medium's eyes as his/her soul is touched - by spirit. It is an indescribable spiritual experience and has a lasting effect upon the medium.

So Spirit Guides look like, and bring the feelings, we associate with Angels but we must allow the beings who glory in the name of Angels, and who are close to the Godhead, the freedom to carry out the celestial tasks assigned to them. As mediums we can rejoice in the fact that we are blessed with the friendship and love of our Spirit Guides who to us, are our personal guardian angels.

ANIMAL GUIDES

I am told by many people that they get a lot of pleasure, comfort and love when they share their home with an animal, usually a dog or a cat. These people are naturally very distressed when one of their pets dies. Its physical presence is no longer with them and this is very sad. What is even sadder, however, is when they, and mediums, start attributing human qualities to these pets once they have 'crossed that great divide'.

Not only has it been known for mediums to purport to link with animals and give messages to the owners but also, reports of these wonderful returns have been given coverage in the psychic press. It is very disconcerting to read that a dog is telling its owner, via the medium, that he understands why she took him to the Vet for that nasty operation!?? I think, at times, Spiritualists ask for all the flak that they receive.

I think the reasoning behind this is due to the fact that we are told communication in the world of spirit is normally carried out by thought. It would logically follow, therefore, that as animals think, mediums will be able to link into their thoughts and bring forward any message the animal wishes to be relayed to its owner. This I think is flawed reasoning for the simple fact that animals may be able to think but they do not have the same logical, reasoning, thinking powers that humans have. They respond to the love, care and attention we give them and can appear at times to be highly intelligent but we must take into account the heightened senses animals have. What may sometimes seem mystical to us can be reasonably explained by the fact that the animal's sense of smell, or eyesight is far greater than ours.

Having said the above, however, it is still very comforting to be given a message from a medium that your pet has been brought in by the communicating spirit, as its love for you remains constant.

Apart from receiving messages from pets, however, this love of them extends to elevating them to Guide status. This is a fascinating theory if we take into account the fact that many humans who wish to train as Guides will spend a long time (in Earth values of time) in that training, while animals can become a Guide upon transition. What is even more odd is that not just pets can be guides, but evidently all animals, birds or even crawling reptiles can achieve such elevated status. This, I feel, comes about by the confusion of two religions and/or sacred disciplines, i.e. Spiritualism and Shamanism.

In Shamanism people can be advised of their totem animals or do journeys on which they will discover these animals. A totem animal is symbolic of an attribute a person already has or is working towards, e.g. if a Grey Wolf represents Teacher, then Teachers and those aspiring or studying to become Teachers will find that one of their totem animals is a Grey Wolf. In Shamanism, on these journeyings, the totem animals apparently are able to give voice and speak directly to the Shaman or novitiate.

Having done one or two journeyings, I see very little, if any, difference between a journeying and a visualisation exercise; the power of the mind, or imagination, is applied and the traveller follows the directions given by the Group Leader or invents his own pathway to follow. As far as I am concerned, therefore, it follows that any animal you may think you see has been put there by your own imagination, and/or your own spirit, and any messages, which such animals may give to you, come direct from that source - yourself or your own inner spirit.

Let us not mix up Spiritualism and Shamanism, even though there are many aspects of each similar to the other. Let us also not misunderstand the symbology of totem animals and their place in the enhancement of psychic and/or mediumistic abilities.

Animals do not speak! Spiritualist Mediums do not have Animal Guides!

I am including here a question and answer found in the book Extemporaneous Addresses. In this book, one of Spiritualism's well-known and well-loved pioneering medium, Emma Hardinge Britten is questioned at the Winter Soirees which were held in Harley Street, London; the date of this soiree being 8 January 1866.

QUESTION

Animals have brains and nervous systems, and exhibit phenomena, mental, moral, and emotional, which seem to differ only in degree from those of human life: they think, they reason, and invent novel and ingenious methods of attaining their objects, of overcoming their difficulties and remedying evils; they also manifest, love, hatred, gratitude, revenge, joy, grief, jealousy, etc., and have also methods of communication with each other. In our superior human nature we regard these as manifestations of the spirit within us, acting through the machinery of the brain and nervous system, and we know that spirit to survive the death of our mortal part. What is it that produces these analogous, though inferior manifestations in the brute creation, and what becomes of it after their death?

ANSWER

"The first Question presented requires us to define the difference between instinct and reason. It has been claimed, and justly, that the higher order of animals have a nervous system, whilst even the lower orders, in some form or other, are provided with an apparatus for the diffusion of nervous sensibility, correspondential to a system, excepting such forms of life as the mollusca, or other rudimental creatures, up to the humble worm, which exhibits a chain of ganglions, terminating in the larger one called the brain. Ranging up from the lower order of animals to the highest, we find a gradual improvement in the complexity of the nervous system, which is the apparatus which thought traverses: it is the telegraphic wire upon

which the life-lightning's play, and without it the
most magnificent and boundless scope of thought
can never exhibit itself in matter. Consequently it is
with especial reference to the nervous system, as a
physical cause, that we must first attempt to answer
your Question

We find that even the lowest orders of being
exhibit a degree of instinct which is admirably
appropriate to their condition. All the creatures of
the dry land or of the water possess instincts adapted
to their state: the reptile and the amphibious
creature, fish and cold-blooded animals, generally
are, if not fully provided with the same complex
system of nerves as the mammalia, still organised
with special arrangements for the generation of just
the amount of vitality adapted to their state, and
subservient to the instincts peculiar to that state. Yet
the amount of instinct thus exhibited has never yet
been classed as reason. It is, then, between the
mammalia, as the highest order of animals, and man,
that we must endeavour to draw the chief distinction
between instinct and reason, and the question
assumes a still more subtle form when we remember
that the highest order of mammalia possesses a
nervous system almost equal to that of man. In them,
too, we find the heart, with its arterial and venous
apparatus for the distribution of the circulating
fluids, as elaborately developed as in the human
form. We find that the brain, although it differs in
quantity in different creatures, is almost as complex
in its structure and convolutions as that of man: but
we also find that the great column of the nervous
system – the spine – with its ganglionic termination
of the brain, is disposed differently in the animal to
that of the man. In the animal it runs laterally with

23

the ground, and the brain receives the galvanic power of the solar ray at an angle which varies considerably from the direct or perpendicular. Man, on the contrary, in his erect position, receives the first direct impetus from the solar ray in the action of a horizontal beam; hence, whatever force the power of light and heat can exercise upon receptive forms, have in this attitude full scope for their exhibition, and must form a line of demarcation between the play of nervous force in the human and in the mammalia thus differently stimulated. And the next evidence of difference in degree of nervous force exhibited in form, is found in the fact that no single form in creation is capable of exhibiting the same amount of intellectual power as man. Whilst the eagle's wing can bear him upward to the sun, the power of man can transcend the eagle's flight in the mechanical powers of mind displayed in the balloon. The mole can mine; the beaver build; the ant and bee manifest the united power of the geometrician and mathematician; the wasp's and the tarantula's nests are models of self-taught architecture: in short, throughout the whole range of natural history, every creature manifests a peculiarity of instinct which antedates human inventions, and emulates, in every form, the genius of man. But let it be remembered that these evidences of mental power are only exhibited in the lower creatures in one or two directions at a time. The animals which seem capable by training of enlarging the sphere of their faculties are very rare, and it is only in creatures which become the companions of, and are subject to, the intellect of man, that we realise the qualities set forth in your statement.

The instincts necessary to the preservation and perpetuation of species are manifest in all living creatures alike, for instance; the love that protects their young and associates gregariously in species and tribes. The manifestations of love, hatred, jealousy, revenge, prevision, and caution; all these are displayed in every species; but their exercise is limited within its species, and comprehends nothing outside of its own nature. All species realise others antagonistic to them; comprehend that which forms appropriate aliment, confine themselves within their own element, yet seem to comprehend the creatures on whom they can prey or consociate with; but none of the lower kingdom manifest evidence of an intellect outside of their own limited and defined form. Thus the building beaver, the geometrical ant, the weaving spider, and the hunting buffalo, are wonderfully instructive only in the direction of that one peculiar attribute which their form implies. The keen scent of the hound, the wonderful instincts of the migrating bird and of the hibernating animal, and even the prophetic power which teaches these creatures to lay up stores against the approaching seasons of scarcity - all this which looks so very like the action of calculating reason, when analytically considered, resolves itself at last into a necessity which grows out of the anatomy of all these creatures, and without now entering into detail, I affirm that each one is not only peculiarly adapted for the manifestation of the instinct it displays, but is as much compelled to exercise that instinct as the necessity of its form, as the flower must needs give off peculiar fragrance, and fruits or roots their quality or essence. It is far otherwise in the organism of man: this is mobile in every conceivable direction. Could the span of human life and strength, extend to the physical exertion, the foot of man is capable of compassing the earth; while the power of intellect enables him to traverse it by mechanical means without the waste of time and strength either on land or air or ocean. The wild beast of the forest is unfitted for the habitations of rock. The savage tenants of the cave subsist not in the field or pasture in the meadow. Each creature is fitted only for the soil and scene in which it is found, nor has any individual of a species, instincts which direct it to enter upon any other element, scene, or sphere of action than its own. But how various and infinitely subtle are the instincts whose assemblage we call reason in man! The throbbing pulse, like the wonderful indicator of the steam-engine, records the quantity and energetic action of the fires of life. Each organ works a telegraphic chain of nerves which informs the brain how much fatigue or effort man may make - how much emotion mind can well endure. The beast may feel all passions you describe, as love or hate or jealousy, or any of those feelings called emotions, yet is unable by any telegraph between the heart and the brain to determine how far its power must be controlled by judgment, intellect, or reason. It ever acts in the peculiar direction of its passions, and knows no hindrance to their play but physical exhaustion. Throughout the whole range of the human organism there is an adaptability to every circumstance; while the reason of man knits up into one, all the fragments of intellectual power that are manifest in every other creature. Thus man is a spinner, weaver, builder, engineer, and navigator. With the mariner's compass he is enabled to guide his course over the pathless wastes of ocean better than the migratory instincts of even the swallow or the martin: by his intellect he is enabled to calculate atmospheric changes, and to determine even centuries hence what shall be the physical aspects of nature, from what they now exhibit by the observation of the growth and formation of strata beneath his feet. There is not an element of mind, nor an atom of matter, but what is subject to man, and combined in his organism. There is not an element of mind or an atom of matter, but what is *distributed* amongst the animal creation, but only in diverse forms and scattered fragments; whilst therefore we find the parts of being divided in them, in man we behold them all combined as in creation's microcosm.

Then arise the questions which I would fain elaborate more fully, were there not so many other subjects of interest to consider. What shall become of this sovereign spirit of man, the totality of all other spiritual entities? And what of the fragments which constitute the life and instinct of the animal creation? Ask the realm of nature how she deals with the perfect and imperfect, the parts and whole of being. There we find that whatsoever is perfect is preserved, while imperfection pays sins wages - death, and passes as a fragment into higher forms to constitute a whole. Hence, while every animal is perfect in its degree, it is not perfect in relation to the highest of forms, which is man. It is only perfect as regards its own peculiar state and sphere. Here upon this earth, its being is necessary, its place is marked; but man, to whom the earth and all things of it are subjects, transcends the earth, and, therefore, belongs to spheres higher than earth. It is sometimes claimed at the spirit circle that all the forms known in the animal kingdom are found in the spirit-spheres. And this is true of some spheres which contain all types of earth and which preserve the representations of every condition manifested here, from the lowest mollusca to the highest man. You can annihilate nothing, therefore you cannot annihilate the fragments of thought which vitalise and move the very humblest form; but such forms are not preserved in permanent immortality, because they are not perfect, nor susceptible of continuing an individualised existence any longer than the form which it occupies is useful to creation, therefore, though for a time in the eternal progress of things the animal forms are preserved in something like a spiritual representative shape, these at last become extinct. Even as the monsters which are no longer useful to the earth's surface have now become extinct and passed away, so for a time in the lower spheres you will find the representative forms of animals preserved, but not in the higher. There, where the perfected spirit of man dwells there is no consociation with animal forms whatsoever. We claim that the animal spirit, then, has a continued but not an immortal existence, whilst the spirit of man, as the perfect elaboration of form, the elaboration of intellect, the cosmos that binds up all of existence known or conceived of in the universal mind - this remains forever. The imperfect dies; the beautiful and perfect never."

We now have the choice as to whether or not we accept this explanation given by one of the spirit guides of Emma Hardinge-Britten, who was possibly one of the greatest mediumistic pioneers of Modern Spiritualism. I choose to do so even though I have been given a message by a medium that my squirrel guide, busy brushing my hair at the time, was telling me I was beautiful. While I can accept the words (can't we all) I will never accept animal guides and even were there such guidance available to me, I would reject it. I wish to communicate with people of the same, or even higher, reasoning powers than myself and I am afraid that no one will be able to convince me that animals can achieve this, beautiful and loving though they may be.

I find it sad, and perhaps oddly touching, that people who have become aware of spirit and mediumship and how it affects their own lives can be very dogmatic when the answers to their questions do not conform with what they wish the answers to be. On a personal level I cannot see the point in asking spirit guides questions if you are not prepared to consider the answers given. There can be conflicting answers from guides and this can often be laid at the feet of the mediums. Far too often mediums go public with their trance mediumship before it is developed to the level to connect with the teaching guides and withstand the pressure and often, unfavourable conditions, in a public meeting. As a rule of thumb I tend to accept answers when they are being repeated by many well-known guides such as Silver Birch, Ramadhan, Red Cloud etc.

We do not change when we move back into spirit and neither will our pets so let us treat them as such – creatures given to us to love and protect which is always a two-way process.

AURAS
(mending and cleansing thereof)

While the literature on the aura and its composition are prolific there are still some people who are convinced that it can tear, have holes in it or even leak energy. It also follows that these same people are well qualified to do the necessary repairs to the aura.

All the teachings from Spirit Guides tell us that the aura, or human atmosphere, is mainly electro-magnetic in composition and surrounds the body like a vortex of energy. The aura is not physical in nature inasmuch as, although it can be felt by those sensitive to its vibrations, its molecular structure is not the same as that, say in a door which is solid to the touch and objects cannot be passed through it. The atomic structure of the aura would perhaps be similar to the noble gases, i.e. oxygen, hydrogen etc which we know exist but cannot be seen with the naked eye.

Taking the above into account then, it can be seen that it is physically impossible for an energy field to have a tear in it, like a piece of torn material. It would need to be of a solid structure for this to take place. The aura is said to be a reflection of its owner. I would perhaps liken it to the subconscious mind as everything that has ever happened in our lives is registered there and psychics can link into it and feedback information that can be quite astounding to psychically unaware people. As well as containing all our life's history - our joys, sorrows and our personality, it reflects that information in various colours and shades to which a psychic and/or medium can attune and become aware of the information these colours reflect.

There are numerous excellent books written on the aura, possibly one of the most interesting being The Aura by Dr W J Kilner, a Doctor from St Thomas Hospital, who used dycyanine to coat glass, which, when looked through, showed the aura. Dr Kilner wasn't interested in reading the colours or giving personality profiles from them. He was able to use his research into the auric field to detect potential illnesses in his patients.

(There is
(No Tears in
auras)

Many people have been very distressed by being told by so-called psychics and/or mediums, that they have tears in the aura or part of it is leaking energy. I know of one poor soul who spent much time in a Psychiatric Hospital because of her fears regarding her holey aura. She was frightened because she thought an 'evil spirit' could invade her body using this hole! She became quite paranoid about this and no amount of reassurance or explanation of the aura's nature was of any help whatsoever; she had convinced herself she was in serious trouble and that is naturally what happened.

The good news is (and I am afraid I am now being sarcastic!) that you can buy an Aura Repair Kit from some of the Psychic Fayres which is basically a needle and thread costing £60. Isn't modern technology wonderful?

I am also at a loss to understand how people who claim to be able to get rid of these holes in auras for people actually do it, taking into account, as always, that it is not a solid structure.

As I understand the aura, illness, or potential illness, within a person, or perhaps negative thinking, can create dark and murky colours in it. If this is the case then only recovery from the illness and/or a change of attitude is going to get rid of these dark patches. One way I can think of in which other people can be of assistance with this problem is to give healing which will help any illness reflecting through the aura.

It would be a little difficult I would think to actually establish where any such holes are within the aura, taking into account the fact that the aura contains many levels. There is not just one aura. The levels range from 5 or 6 to the ridiculous. Listed below are three of these lists of comprehensive aura levels which were discovered courtesy of the internet. In all these lists number 1 is the aura closest to the physical body and considered to be the lowest level.

LIST ONE

1. Physical auric body - Physical sensations. Simple physical comfort, pleasure, health.
2. The etheric auric body - Emotions with respect to self. Self-acceptance and self love.
3. Vital auric body - Rational mind. To understand the situation in a clear, linear, rational way.
4. Astral (emotional) body - Relations with others. Loving interaction with friends and family.
5. Lower mental auric body - Divine will within. To align with the divine will within, to make commitment to speak and follow the truth.
6. Higher mental auric body - Divine love, and spiritual ecstasy.
7. Spiritual (intuitive) body - Divine mind, serenity. To be connected to divine mind and to understand the greater universal pattern.

LIST TWO

1. The etheric layer.
2. The emotional layer.
3. The mental layer.
4. The astral layer.
5. The etheric template layer.
6. The celestial layer.
7. The ketheric layer.

LIST THREE

1. Physical Plane – Physical Plane, Etheric, physical.
2. Emotional Plane – Astral Plane.
3. Mental Plane – Manasic Plane, conscious mind.

4. Intuitional Plane – Buddhic Plane, Higher mental.
5. Spiritual Plane – Atmic Plane, etheric template first spiritual.
6. Monadic Plane – Anupadaka Plane, celestial – second spiritual.
7. Divine Plane – Adi Plane or Plane of the Logos. Ketheric.

It can be seen from the above three lists that people really are not too sure what the various levels are or even what is the correct name for them. Within Spiritualism we tend to speak of only four levels while acknowledging there will be other levels that we are not necessarily aware of, or need to know about.

These levels are:
1. Physical
2. Mental
3. Emotional
4. Spiritual

It seems that most of the lists are not in agreement with respect to the levels used within Spiritualism so perhaps it is us who are out of step with everyone else.

When researching these various levels I was very interested in the word 'ketheric' not having come across it before and evidently the word means The Divine Level. What does concern me, however, is the following quotation from a book by Barbara Brennan, and is with respect to healing these different auric levels.

"Healing the ketheric template. Organ restructuring: The hands of the healer "remove the ketheric field of the organ, the organ then floats above the body where it is cleaned and restructured by more rapid finger movements." (Brennan, 222) Chakra restructuring: Threads of "gold light pour out of your

hands... sewing the small vortex in [the] chakra."
(Brennan, 225) - *I knew the aura repair kit would come in useful.*

One thing we have to realise when discussing colours and levels of the aura is that it is not possible to scientifically prove its existence. Many mediums will look at the same person's aura and see different colours and also give different meanings for these colours. We can understand why this could happen, due to the different auric levels, but this would not be acceptable to a scientist.

There is also a great deal of interest in the 'Aura Cameras' which are on the market at the moment which claim to photograph the colours within the aura – but again, at which level? Physical? Mental: Emotional? Spiritual? People tend to accept them as genuine when they are given a personality reading from the photograph. This same reading could be given using tarot cards, rune stones, ribbons etc. the photograph is only a focus for a psychic reading.

I do know, from personal experience, that some results of experimentation with these cameras, have been quite startling but I do feel a lot more experiments need to be undertaken before any claims can be made that the colours shown on the photographs are those of the aura.

We do not know enough about the composition and different levels of the aura. Psychics and mediums, therefore, should be extremely careful when talking about it. They should always ensure that nothing is ever said which could frighten the person to whom they are speaking

CALLING UP THE DEAD

There appear to be quite a few mediums working who ask that the sitter give them a name or a relationship to concentrate upon in order for them to 'summon' that person to come and communicate with the sitter. The question must, therefore, be asked:

'Can a medium call up any particular spirit person'

The short answer is: NO! Definitely not.

It is not possible to demand that people in this life be at your beck and call and for them to do as you wish, so why should it be any different in the Spirit World. The whole thrust of the messages which come back to us through the agency of mediumship is that people do not change when they move into the Spirit World. They have only left their physical body behind which was only a vehicle of expression for the spirit while living in a physical world. It certainly is not required in the Spirit World.

If the personality of the person who has now returned to the Spirit World is the same as it was on earth then a stubborn, obstinate person will ignore any 'calls' or 'summonses' from people living on this earth. Mediums do not have any extraordinary power which would facilitate such an event. Any mediums who promise that they are capable of bringing forward a designated spirit person is not only fooling the people wishing to hear from loved ones in the Spirit World, but they are also fooling themselves.

It must be said, however, that family and friends now living in Spirit are aware of how much we love and miss them and will do everything within their power to make contact when they can, but it will always be their choice.

It has been known for many sitters, who are newly bereaved, to attend for a private sitting with the thought of only one person in mind. They are advised very gently to keep an open mind because mediums cannot promise to be able to contact any one particular person. Notwithstanding this, the sitter can still only focus on that one person as they are desperately seeking contact with him or her. What I find particularly uplifting is that the desired person very often is able to make contact and bring the comfort and support to the family member that is needed.

There are also a few requirements for a contact to be made. The medium must be developed to a level where they can link into the vibrations of the Spirit World; conditions, such as negativity and scepticism can create barriers to communication as can depleted energy levels; these conditions can cause interference so any message will not be clear.

Spirit certainly will make contact, if invited and if the conditions are such that they are able to do so, but to demand or summon any one soul is demeaning, discourteous and not worthy of any medium worth his or her salt.

To take this a step further, the question should be asked: "Can spirit summon up the living?"

There are some people who are of the opinion that anyone who has developed mediumship to the level of clear communication, has a responsibility to their guides/helpers/spirit world to be available 24/7.

There are stories told of people being awoken by spirit in the early hours of the morning. They do not recognize the spirit, they do not know who the recipient of any spirit communication is to be, and yet they are happy for such contact to be made.

Can I say, first of all, that I do not believe spirit wake us up; I cannot see my parents (in spirit) being happy if my sleep was disturbed and I would expect my guides to prevent such disturbance. What I do think can, and does, happen, is that sometimes when we wake during the night and are still in that lovely floaty state – in between sleep and full wakefulness – some spirits may draw close and take advantage of the fact that we are possibly at our most receptive, and enter into communication with us. This would only happen, as far as I am concerned, to people who have indicated that they are happy for it to happen. It would never happen to me unless it was an emergency and then I would, just as I am sure everyone else would, be happy to assist in whatever way I could.

Communication, therefore, is not about demands, orders, summonses from either side of life - it is about co-operation.

In conclusion: free will becomes a nonsense if it is possible for spirit people to be dragged from whatever they are doing by a medium and made to 'perform'. The whole idea is laughable. The dead may also try to summon a medium but a medium who is in control of his of her mediumship will only respond if that is what is wished. There is free will on both sides of life.

CHAKRAS

The word chakra, is a Sanskrit word and translates as 'wheel'. Chakras are said to appear to people who can see them as spinning wheels of coloured light. These centres, and their interconnecting pathways (meridians) were charted by the Chinese, Indians and other Eastern races, thousands of years ago. Modern versions of these charts are still widely used today, in many types of alternative medicine and body work, i.e., acupuncture and reflexology.

These whirling vortices of energy are said to comprise the psycho-physical bridge which link the physical part of the human body to its energy source which Buddhists call Prana. Prana is the life force and this energy is drawn into the physical body through the chakras, or energy centres.

A chakra can be likened to a transformer. For reasons of efficiency, electricity is delivered through the national grid at a very high voltage. However, this voltage is too high to deliver directly to a house. Apart from being dangerous to the house it would burn out any appliance connected directly to it. To resolve this, transformers are used to step down the high voltage from the national grid to the correct voltage for the appliances in our homes. In a similar way the chakra steps down the high vibration of power around us to a level suitable for our bodies. Each chakra steps down the power to a different level or vibration which is needed for the organs and glands which it feeds.

The number of chakras the human body has seems to vary from 7 to 88,000 dependent upon the knowledge and experiences of the various authors providing the information. It is also said that the energy transformed through these chakras re-energises the body and then flows from it as the auric envelope. If this is true then every pore on a human body must be a chakra of some description. It is accepted, however, that there are seven main chakras and perhaps knowing the actual number of all the energy centres required by the human body is not as important as is often thought to be the case.

If the abundant information mankind has regarding chakras is correct, taking into account that some of it goes back thousands of years and mainly stems from Eastern philosophies and to dismiss it would be foolish, how does this affect mediums and Spiritualists?

It is a fact that some novice mediums are still being trained to 'open' these chakras in order to become attuned to spirit and to 'close' them when they are finished their spirit work.

This does not make sense to me for the following reasons:

1. If these energy centres are our connection to the life force and we were able to close them, then we

would, in effect, be closing ourselves off from this force; in short we would be dead.

2. My understanding of the development of mediumship is that novice mediums sit in circles to allow their spirit guides to help unfold their mediumistic potential.

There are many excellent mediums working in Spiritualist Churches who have developed their mediumship without having any knowledge of the chakra system whatsoever so to say that mediums need to open them is certainly not true.

It is also said that these energy centres can become blocked and need to be cleansed and balanced. Firstly I am not too sure how they can become blocked but perhaps negativity and depressing thoughts can cause an imbalance. If that is the case then I am still at a loss to understand how 'waving' a crystal over them can rid anyone of negativity and/or depressing thoughts. Only the individual concerned can do that and I would have thought that spirit healing is more likely to have a beneficial effect than anything else.

If, as it is claimed, these are energy centres keeping us topped up, as it were, I am not sure which type of energy they bring to us. They do not give us physical energy as we get that from food; so it has to be emotional energy, mental energy, intellectual energy and/or spiritual energy. Again I have problems as I cannot see that any amount of cleansing, balancing etc is going to make any person more intellectual than they currently are. I am also not sure that I would want my emotional levels any higher than at the present and, can chakra cleansing make an individual more spiritual?

There are too many claims regarding chakras made in the West by people who do not have the knowledge and understanding of them, as do the Gurus and Teachers of the Eastern philosophies.

If they are important in the development of mediumship, and that may well be the case, then I am sure we can leave it to our spirit guides to carry out any required procedures with respect to them.

As far as I am concerned, living a healthy, active life and trying to remain positive at all times will do our little 'wheels of life' far more good than any crystal cleansing, dowsing, Tibetan bowls or colour meditations.

CHANNELLING

Definitions of Channelling:
"The process by which a medium can communicate information from non-physical beings, such as spirits, deities, demons or aliens through entering a state of trance or some other form of altered consciousness".[1]

"Central to a lot of New Age beliefs is the practice of "channelling". This is not a new practice, however, but rather, Spiritualism with a modern title. In this practice the person involved in the channelling allows him/herself to be taken over by a spirit, an angel, deceased guru or wise man, or even an alien being.

It is interesting to observe the consistent pattern that emerges in channelling from spirits, the deceased, and alien entities. Most messages speak of the following themes: reincarnation, and the teaching that humans are gods. Jesus is usually seen as just a wise teacher who was one of many, and the Bible is usually regarded as untrustworthy.

---

[1] Dictionary of The Occult

If you want to know what these beings look like, you will find that they have very kindly allowed, not only their messages to be channelled, but also their images as well. This is seen in the many channelled images and paintings created by those who have allowed themselves to be open to spirit entities. Such images are commonly seen in New Age Fairs."[1]

This site is Christian so it is very easy to spot the bias contained upon the site.

What is Channelling?

As far as I am concerned, the word channelling has been introduced into the occult and Spiritualist language over the past 20 years and people are often confused as to what it actually means.

Channelling is the ability to obtain information from personalities who do not live on earth. Mediums do this when they use their sensitivity to link into spirit vibrations and, using either clairvoyance, clairaudience or clairsentience, or a combination of all three, bring forward evidence from a spirit communicator which is relevant to the recipient of such a communication.

Channelling is also used to describe what is more normally known as trance mediumship. The state of trance is an altered state of consciousness which can vary from a very slight overshadowing of the medium's mind by a spirit operator, to a very deep level of control. In this latter state the medium's consciousness is suppressed to such a degree that he or she has no memory of any occurrences during the period the control was taking place.

Mediums who enter the trance state allow the spirit operator, usually one of their guides, to take control of their body, especially the voice box, thereby enabling the

---

[1] www.spotlightministries.org.uk

spirit control to speak to sitters and give spirit teachings or evidence of survival. This does not mean that the spirit guide enters the medium's body - control can be effected from quite a distance.

Some Channellers claim to bring through beings from other planets and alien universes. Claims of this kind should be considered in the light of any accompanying evidence. Without such evidence, these claims will never be given serious consideration by investigating scientists who are earnestly seeking evidence of survival of humans after the change called death. They are also very interested in information regarding other life forms but again, validation would be required.

There is actually one website (www.sonic.net/~marina/) where the site owner claims to have channelled all the Ascended Masters, including Jesus, oh and by the way, God came through as well!

Something I find very strange with channelling is that it can be taught and usually doesn't take long before contact has been made and someone is being channelled through.

Mediums sitting for trance can sit for months, years perhaps and even after the breakthrough takes place it can still take a long time before the medium will go public - not so with channellers, so perhaps there is a clear difference between channelling and trance.

Channellers are very closely linked to Spiritualism as many claim to be mediums and Spiritualists. It is apparent, therefore, that all Trance Mediums and Channellers should be very careful who they allow to control and speak through them as there is a very real danger that they could inadvertently be instrumental in bringing discredit to the very people they purport to represent.

CHILDREN

There has been a lot of talk for the last few years about children being saviours of the world and in the main, these children are the Indigo Children, many of whom are now adults. Now I am not certain, at this stage, whether these children are being considered to have been produced within, or by, Spiritualists, but because of their emphasised psychic natures, perhaps it is better that we try and gain an understanding of them. Many people will assume that they are part of Spiritualism and that perhaps many of our young mediums are Indigo Children.

A trawl of the Internet has produced the following, which is the tiniest tip of the iceberg as there is so much information on this subject:

"Indigo children is a concept developed by Nancy Anne Tappe describing children who are alleged to possess special traits or abilities. Beliefs about indigo children range from their being the next stage in human evolution, possessing paranormal abilities such as telepathy, to the belief that they are simply more empathetic and creative than their non-indigo peers. There is no science or studies that give credibility to the existence or traits of indigo children. Many children labelled "indigo" are diagnosed with attention-deficit hyperactivity disorder.

Skeptics suggest that the indigo phenomenon is due to parents preferring to believe their children are special, rather than having a medical diagnosis which implies damage or imperfection. Also criticized are the traits used to describe children, which have been compared to the Forer effect - so vague as to be able to apply to anyone.

The concept was initially developed in the 1970s, gaining popular interest with the publication of a series of books in the late 1990s and the release of several films in the following decade. A variety of books, conferences and related materials have been created surrounding the idea of indigo children, which have been criticized for a means of making money from credulous parents."[1]

It can be seen from the above that Indigo Children are just an idea! A concept by Nancy Tappe and that there is no scientific evidence for the claims she makes. No one, to date, can prove the colours in anyone's aura so what this lady has done, as far as I am concerned, is very cruel. The families of children who have been diagnosed with problems such as ADHD have enough to deal with without being given false hope. I am sure these people don't really need to be told that their children are special, they already know that, and it has nothing whatsoever to do with being psychic.

It seems that the Indigo Children gave birth to the Crystal Children and, as with the Indigo Children, there is much information regarding them on the Internet:

"The Crystal Children are those born from the year 1995 and later and they have the most beautiful big eyes. They appear angelic in looks and their eyes appear to see right through you. These children, like the Indigos are here to save the world and they know just how to do it. These children are happy, delightful and forgiving. Also like the Indigos they are highly sensitive and psychic and they have important life purposes. The main difference from the Indigos is their temperament. While the Indigo

---

[1] www.wikipedia.org

child have a warrior spirit and the Crystal child is blissful and even tempered. They do have tantrums occasionally, but these children are largely forgiving and easy going.

The term Indigo child and Crystal child were given to these children because it most accurately describes their aura colours and energy patterns. While Indigos have a lot of indigo blue in the auras (which is the third eye chakra colour), the Crystals have beautiful, multicoloured, opalescent auras, in pastel hues like a quartz crystals prism effect. This generation of children will also harbour a fascination for crystals and rocks. The Crystals also have magnetic personalities, they can start talking late in childhood, are very musically orientated and may sing before they talk. They also use telepathy and self-invented sign language to communicate. They are also very connected to nature and animals and they will discuss their past lives and will see Angels, Spirit and Guides. They are extremely artistic and creative and they prefer vegetarian food and juices to regular food. They will be fearless explorers and climbers with an amazing sense of balance."[1]

Reading the qualities of what makes a crystal child different to other children is confusing as all those qualities, with the exception of the auric reading which is unsubstantiated, can be found in all children everywhere and always has been.

The Crystal Children are followed by the Rainbow Children (wonder who comes next?) and the information on these was taken from an angel therapy site:

---

[1] www.mystic familiar.com

"Meet the Rainbow Children!

They are the embodiment of our divinity and the example of our potential. The Rainbow Children have never lived on this planet before, and they're going straight to the Crystal Children as their moms and dads. These children are entirely fearless of everybody. They're little avatars who are all about service. These are children who are only here to give - Rainbow Children are already at their spiritual peak.

These children are the answers to our prayers.

The Rainbow Children are now being born as the Crystal Children become adults. And these are a few adult Crystal Children that are in their 20s now. Rainbow Children are coming about because the full spectrum of light that we need to assimilate serotonin in our body has been reduced. In other words, when we go out on a clear day with no smog and we're out in the sunshine, we're receiving in our body a "rainbow" through the sun waves. And that's the way that we were created - to need rainbow energy."[1]

I think we have to discount Rainbow Children totally because of the mathematics. If their mums and dads are the adult Crystal Children who were born 1995 and after, then those same Crystal Children are only 14 (2009) now. Perhaps these children have not been born yet and we can look forward to receiving them into our world.

My next offering from the Internet is a transcript of a guide of Daniel Jacobs talking about an even newer race of people who are going to save the world:

---

[1] www.angeltherapy.com

"My Dear Friends,

Now is a time of great stress and activation upon the Earth! And there are even greater activations yet to come. It is for this reason that we approach you once again, in our usual shared space of remembrance and fond communion.

The Spirit of the Oneself is now calling forth all those who have been cloaked in limitation, or sleeping in separation, to ARISE--and to take on those tones of illumination that are their birthright, their legacy. And you who receive this message, in whatever form it comes, may consider yourself to be one with them--and also invited--regardless of past experience or chronological age. For the herald comes now to each, in his or her best familiar language and sacred circumstance. And there is no favouritism required. All are called, and all are welcome. But not all will respond. And that, too, has its resonance.

In our transmission "Neo-Shamans of the New Millennium," we spoke to you about a group of individuals, who have been strategically placed, all over the globe, to be of help to humanity when the intense changes begin to happen. Of these individuals, we said the following:

"These are the Children of Oneness, aged and seasoned to meet the need which shall surely soon present itself! Though they were born "from the old ways" and steeped in ancient customs and bygone disciplines, they return today to stand beneath the Tree of Life. As thunder rolls and temporary chaos shakes the Tree, these wise and wondrous beings shall catch the ripe fruit, precisely where it falls."

At the time of that transmission, we made no differentiation in the Neo-Shamans, except that they were quite gifted, and they would come in very handy during the upcoming planetary shifts, as your planet moves closer and closer to conscious collective access to the Fourth Dimension.

In times past . . . . you may have received information regarding certain soul groups--called by various names, and distinguished by certain skills and innate abilities. They are found most among your young people. Whether they are referred to as Indigo Children, Crystal Children, Psychic or Star Children, or by whatever name, the CHILDREN OF ONENESS are now awakening--and soon, the rest of humanity will begin awakening with them![1]

Not too certain what to call this last group. Neo-Shamans? Star Children or perhaps Children of Oneness.

What seems to be coming through loud and clear with the qualities and abilities of all these saviour children is the word psychic. Do the writers of the articles not realise that everyone is psychic? When children first come to the earth, their psychic and mediumistic ability is very pronounced. Some then go on to live their lives ignoring it; some allow it lay dormant and then start working with it later in life and for a few, they use these abilities right throughout their lives. Really we have not been told anything new.

- Children are Psychic! Yes we know
- Children are Special! Yes we know
- Children can save the world! That potential has always been there. They are our future.

While it would be nice to think that the world can be diverted from the destructive path it appears to be upon at

---

[1] www.reconnections.net

the moment, it is illogical to think that it will be, what is in the main, special needs children who will do it. Don't these children have big enough problems to deal with without placing the sins of the world upon their shoulders?

So let us allow our children to grow in peace and make their own choices when they feel they are ready. Until that day comes let us also realise that the only way these children can be part of Spiritualism is by becoming Spiritualists when they are old enough. Spiritualism does not have these various denominations of children within its structure but it will always welcome them into its Churches.

One last point and that is on the make up and construction of the aura (or human atmosphere). It has a lot more levels than we are aware of and every level is pulsating with different colours and we really are a kaleidoscope of colour – a veritable rainbow. I don't need to be given names to feel special, I already know I am and I hope you do too. As a matter of interest I was told many, many years ago that I was a Star Child so according to the literature found on the Internet I haven't arrived on this planet yet. That explains a lot!

CHRISTIANITY
(the trappings of)

Spiritualism is a religion. One of definitions of the word religion is about beliefs and worship: people's beliefs and opinions concerning the existence, nature, and worship of God, a god, or gods, and divine involvement in the universe and human life and Spiritualism certainly falls within this category. There really aren't any legal or moral guidelines as to the format of a religious service and it can be seen by a study of the world's major religions that the coming together for the purpose of worship can take many forms.

It appears within the Spiritualist Church format that a lot has been taken, or copied, from Christianity, e.g. prayers, hymns, readings, an address (sermon), vespers, culminating with a demonstration of mediumship. Many Christian hymns, or tunes, are also used.

If we look at the judgment made in the Law Suit regarding the Church of Scientology which went to a Board of Appeal we will find the following statements relevant:

Every Church that is affiliated to the Spiritualists' National Union, which is a registered Charity and a registered Company, is legally bound by Government and Charity Commissioners' Statutes governing its operation. It is wise, therefore, to bear in mind the comments of a Judge of the Appeal Court when rejecting the appeal of the Scientologists who claimed that their Church was a place of worship.

His comments included the following, relevant to the matter under his discussion:

"It is essential that the building must be truly a place of meeting for religious worship before it can be registered."

"A place of religious worship was one where people come together as a congregation, or an assembly, to do reverence to God. It need not be the God whom Christians worship, it might be another God, or an unknown God, but it must be reverence to a deity."

"The essential to my mind is the nature of worship. When one looks at the ceremony here, i.e. Scientology, the feeling which remains is not one of reverence for God or deity but simply instruction in a philosophy."

Lord Denning was the Judge giving the comments, the Lords Justices Winn and Buckley agreeing. The full

Judgment, together with a letter from the General Secretary of the Union, was circulated throughout the Union, dated 23 July 1970.

It can be seen from this judgment how important it is that the services conducted in any Church can be recognised as religious services and it can also be seen that the format, which is recognised in a Christian country, would be suitable as the basis for the Church Service.

Unfortunately some Churches take it to the extremes. The Churches are filled with Christian artefacts and trappings, so much so that it becomes difficult to understand how an obvious Christian-looking Church can be a Spiritualist one.

It is appreciated that some Spiritualist Churches have acquired Christian Church buildings which come with stained glass windows, fonts and vestries and it is not suggested for a moment that these be ripped out. Perhaps a little thought could be given, however, to removing the Christian elements, as far as is possible, in order to reassure people that they have entered a Spiritualist Church.

We don't need crosses, we don't need Bibles; Spiritualism doesn't have ritual, creed or dogma and any artefacts within the Church suggesting this should be removed.

CLEANSING

Cleansing Houses

When we are discussing cleansing houses it is to rid them of negative energy and I would imagine unwanted spirit entities and/or ghosts. If the problem is spirit then a medium is usually called in who normally doesn't have any other ritual than moving into the silence and establishing communication.

With negative energy, however, there appear to be many methods of doing such cleansing, the most popular being burning sage; sometimes the cleansing is done in the form of a ritual with lighted candles and incense making it all very esoteric.

A search of the Internet gives the following descriptions of how some of the house cleansing exponents carry out their ritual cleansing ceremony. I am only reproducing three out of the many hundreds of sites which offer this service.

"The Process:
I use energy work and counselling of the spirit to cleanse and close down your home. I seal it shut to the spirit world with pure energies so that it is no longer possible for the activity to continue. I make sure that only loved ones from the world of spirit are welcome in your home, or if you prefer, I can seal it completely. If the disturbance is down to a build up of negative energy from the living rather than a spirit person, I can clear that energy too."[1]

"A house may just have a bad feel or it may seem to have a personality which interferes with its current owners and their lives. People may always seem to be ill or have bad luck, in a certain house. A business, such as a pub, may repeatedly fail and go from new owner to new owner with each proprietor sinking all their money and doing nothing wrong. However, the business fails, none the less. It seems inexplicable, after the effort that has been made but, sometimes as rapidly as within a few months, the pub is up for sale again. Spiritual house cleansing can solve this problem.
Some who do this work will come and move on those attachments they are aware of. Mark will

---

[1] www.rachelkeene.co.uk

check the occupiers of the building, first, and deal with any attachments to them. Before starting work on the building, he will seek cooperation from at least one attachment. Then he will start at the boundaries of the property working inwards towards the exterior of the building and finally he will clear the inside of the building."[1]

"I will come first to assess and feel the energies in your home for myself first, to find out if I can pick up on what the trouble is; sometimes I may use a pendulum to help me.
I will then come back at a convenient time for both of us with everything in which I may need.
I use a Tibetan singing bowl, made out of 7 Tibetan metals to cleanse your house in the form of vibrations,
I will then go round a second time with certain incense that are used to dispel negativity, and may go round a third time using a smudging stick, this is using sage bundles and can be a bit Smokey. (This can be left out as not everyone is happy with the smoke)
I will bring and place the most suitable crystals, both for helping to keep future negativity at bay, and for bringing love, light and positive energies into your home.
Sometimes I also use a black and a white candle that you can leave to burn at your leisure, one representing the dispelling of negativity, the other to replace it with positive, and lastly I will show you how to protect your home with salt."[2]

---

[1] www.marksb.info
[2] Michell's Spiritual World

What I have difficulty understanding is who decides the house contains negative energy in the first place. Sometimes if people are experiencing what they feel is bad luck or things are not going the way they would wish, then they appear to have problems accepting that these things actually do happen in life to all of us at some time or another and have nothing whatsoever to do with negative energy. If a family are fighting amongst themselves they often claim it is negative energy making them behave in this manner and not the fact that none of them will compromise and swallow their pride. I feel that the words 'negative energy' are a substitute for the 'devil'. Spiritualists do not accept that there can be a devil but negative energy certainly has its uses!

If there really is negative energy in a house I am still uncertain how burning sage will clear it; is it the smell or the smoke that makes it disappear and can energy disappear? I understand that energy can only transform from one kind to another. Does this energy undergo a transformation and become another form of energy or does it move from the house and take up residence elsewhere? I cannot work out the mechanics of the actual process of cleansing and what does what to what.

After having said all that, it is important to realise that people smudging haunted houses is not what smudging is really all about. Smudging, using herbs and other plants is a Native American ceremony and "Ojibway and Cree ceremonies often use smudges of sage, sweet grass and/or juniper to cleanse with, and to give prayers to the Creator, or Gitche Manitou. Smudges with hot coals underneath can provide a lot of smoke for many hours or days to repel mosquitoes and other insects."[1]

---

[1] Wikipedia

"Smudging is one of the weirder stress-relieving practices to emerge from the US in recent years, but it is charming, harmless and may even be of benefit. It traces its roots to a Native American ceremony, in which you use smoke from burning herbs and incense to cleanse yourself and your surroundings. Smudging derives from the idea that smell is the sense that connects us to a deep, instinctual part of the brain and certain scents have the power to change our energies and trigger emotions. The Savvy Moose website[1] will teach you how to conduct your own ceremony, which usually involves wafting sweet-smelling smoke around yourself and your home with a feather. It will also provide advice on which herbs to use. Sage, for instance, has the power to drive away negative energies. Cedar, juniper and pinon pine provide balance and harmony."[2]

It is not possible, therefore, to dismiss all smudging as unnecessary as to some people, especially Native American Indians, it is a very special ceremony and features a lot in their lives and I, or anyone else for that matter, do not have the right to denigrate their ceremonies. What I do not like are the people who do not have a true understanding of smudging and the kind of cleansing it actually covers.

So how do I deal with negativity in the home, or even around me?

If I walk into a room and am not happy with the atmosphere I encounter then I counteract it by playing beautiful music, put on a favourite video which makes me

---

[1] www.savvymoose.com
[2] www.stressbusting.co.uk

healing

laugh and all wrong feelings soon disappear. Perhaps I have invented another method of cleansing?

SOUL CLEANSING

"A Soul Retrieval Limpia is a soul cleansing and purification performed by a Shaman to help a person become unblocked, healed and protected on many levels."[1]

There then follows a description of such a retrieval which is basically (healing) given by one person at the end of the (telephone) to another.

Some Shamans carry out soul retrieval, which is basically recovering energy. I certainly didn't realise my soul was escaping every time I was drained of energy. The Shaman will take you on a journey (visualisation) where you will meet your totem animal and be rejuvenated, as simple as that.

There is one website I found where the owner states: "As my study of the soul progressed, I quickly noticed the variety of anomalies and problems that can befall the average soul. Attaching spirits, etheric webs, miasms, soul fragments from living and discarnate forms, thought forms, toxic radiation, and a myriad of unseen forces bombard the soul on a daily basis. The soul's inborn defenses are capable of dealing with most of these problems, but for the most part, it is only a matter of time before the soul structure itself is damaged by at least one of the above forces."

His problem regarding the soul was resolved when he met a spirit on the astral plane when he was 'out of his body' who had invented a device that utilised sound to remove attaching spirits. To cut a long story short, he

---

[1] www.vibrantuniverse.com

made a device which emitted high frequency sound waves (evidently attaching spirits run away when they hear them) and now he sells this device so we can remove even the 'most ardent ghost' whatever that might mean.

I would not like to think that any Spiritualist felt it was possible for his or her soul to need retrieval or that it was possible for it to be sullied in such a way as to need cleansing.

The problem, as I see it, is that most Spiritualists, upon awakening to their own inner spirit and inherent divinity become actively interested in many esoteric religions and New Age practices; while Shamanism gives lots of comfort to its followers, it is not part of Spiritualism and should be kept separate. To have an insight into another man's belief system gives a greater understanding of the man but we must keep the lines of demarcation very clear as to what is Spiritualism and what is not.

CRYSTALS AND OTHER GEMSTONES

Most Spiritualists have a love of nature and the products of nature including crystals. Gemstones, like gold and silver, are part of the earth's natural resources and are very beautiful, especially when they have been polished.

Most Spiritualist Churches have a little shop, or table, selling crystals and other little objects and gifts, the sale of which helps boost the Church's finances.

Some Spiritualists and/or mediums have studied crystals and will run workshops using them - they will often also include crystal healing as part of their crystal skills.

A stranger to Spiritualist could be forgiven for thinking that perhaps crystals are part of Spiritualism, especially when crystal readings are being given. In this case the crystals are being used as a focus for a psychic reading just as cards, crystal balls, rune stones etc are used. They can, therefore, be used to assist in the enhancement of the psychic skills of novice mediums which will, in turn, help the development of their mediumship.

The Churches are responsible for providing education in the principles of SNU Spiritualism[1] and this education would naturally include the training of tomorrow's exponents. Bearing this in mind, crystals are still not part of Spiritualism even though they may be used within Churches to achieve one of its objects.

Cards, ribbons, runes etc are used for teaching purposes only; sometimes a Special Evening may be held when a medium, using her psychic skills, will demonstrate working with colour. Should such an event take place the Chairman should explain to the audience exactly what is to happen, stressing that the medium will not be linking to people in the spirit world and that the whole event is in the nature of an experiment. This will ensure there is no confusion in people's minds as to the actual nature of the event.

So crystals and other gemstones, together with other focus tools, may be used in a Spiritualist Church, but are not really part of the Science, Religion and Philosophy of Spiritualism.

DEVILS, DEMONS AND INCUBI

A DEVIL

The question must be asked: Is there a devil?

Not within the Religion of Spiritualism or in any of the teachings received from Spirit.

It is accepted, however, that people do have their own personal 'devils' and in some cases, people within Spiritualism feel they are influenced by 'evil' spirits. This

---

[1] Rules for Churches Rule 1(c)

is usually the outcome of not having a sound knowledge base of their own and, therefore, taking on board, everything they see, hear or read about Spiritualism, mediumship and spirit.

If Spiritualism allowed a devil within its teachings it would effectively remove the Fifth Principle from its Philosophy for Personal Responsibility does not allow for the luxury of an outside source, of any description, on which an individual can offload his or her obligations and responsibilities.

Spiritualists have no devil as a clothes-horse on which to hang their misdemeanours and misdeeds, although some have been known to blame the influence of spirit for their negative behaviour and such assertions should be treated with the contempt they deserve. People are in control of their bodies; people are in control of their emotions; people are in control of their minds and if they cannot control them then they need physical help because there will be a physical cause inherent thereto.

Man must learn to accept responsibility for every thought, every word and every deed which emanates from him; man must also learn to accept responsibility for every thought, every word and every deed which does not emanate from him but which he knows should have been given expression. Too often people will deliberately bury their heads in the sand and refuse to think about situations in which they are involved in the hope that they will go away; people will also remain quiet when they know they should stand, speak and be counted; people will often refrain from taking action in situations where it is apparent there is a need for them so to do. People are responsible for inaction as well as action which makes understanding Personal Responsibility a truly daunting proposition.

Spiritualism is the thinking man's religion and it is a basic requirement that a Spiritualist, while accepting the

Seven Principles, takes on the implications within these Principles, especially that contained in the Fifth Principle - Personal responsibility.

If any reader needs a devil, that's fine, but please do not ever ascribe such a concept to the religion of Spiritualism as there are enough misconceptions regarding it without adding more.

DEMONS

Are there any demons?

Yes, thousands of them and all in the minds of thriller writers and sometimes within the minds of people who have severe mental problems or experience hallucinations, but in Spiritualism, or even in life - NO. Quite categorically NO.

The science, philosophy and religion of Spiritualism is so simple and easy to understand that to start placing within its inner recesses, fantastic creatures such as demons, hobgoblins, vampires and such, all dreamt up by man, would take away its beauty and simplicity. It appears that quite a few people like to experience the thrill of being scared and this is one of the reasons they sit through horror movies and read books of a similar nature and that is fine but we must allow these things to be thought as being part of Spiritualism as it makes our fight for full recognition even more difficult.

INCUBI AND SUCCUBI

These are supposedly the male and female spirits who creep into our beds with us and have sex with us while we sleep, and sometimes when we are awake.

Wikipedia gives us:

"An incubus (plural incubi) is a demon in male form supposed to lie upon sleepers, especially women, in order to have sexual intercourse with them, according to a number of mythological and legendary traditions. Its female counterpart is the succubus. . An incubus may pursue sexual relations with a woman in order to father a child, as in the legend of Merlin. Some sources indicate that it may be identified by its unnaturally large or cold sexual organ. Religious tradition holds that repeated intercourse with an incubus or succubus may result in the deterioration of health, or even death.

Medieval legend claims that demons, both male and female, sexually prey on human beings. They generally prey upon the victim while they are sleeping, though it has been reported that females have been attacked while fully lucid."

Another demon but one which adds to the thrill of being scared and one which, to my mind, is often used to explain a sexual dream which we think we have awoken from but as the dream continues, we feel that everything which is happening is doing so in the physical world.

Spirit contact is mainly on a mental level as spirit live in a totally different dimension to us and when mediums work with them, they do so by linking minds - telepathy. If someone claims they can feel themselves being sexually assaulted by a spirit then it would be through the mind; If the spirit materialised and took on a physical body then everyone present would witness this. I am not aware of any woman who claims to have been assaulted in such a manner submitting herself for a medical examination and if there has been such examinations, what the results were.

So people looking to find devils, demons, incubi, succubi and other things which go bump in the night will not find them in Spiritualism. Spiritualism doesn't threaten its members to keep them in line.

EVIL SPIRITS

Man is a thrill-seeker. Anything or everything is worth experimenting with in an effort to achieve such thrills. The age old question of 'Why do men climb mountains' is always answered with 'Because they are there'. That may very well be a truth, but it is also true that the potential for danger, and ergo thrills, when climbing a mountain is enormous and therein lies the fascination.

Fairytales and cartoons are filled with scary characters usually chasing each other carrying implements of pain. Are we inadvertently creating this need for stimulation in our children at a very early age. I can still remember my screams of terror, followed by giggles of relief when watching such films (no televisions in my childhood). I can also remember that I did realise it was all fictional and no one really got hurt and that cartoons weren't real people, but that did not stop me from enjoying, and squealing all the way through, Abbott and Costello meet the Ghosts.

As we grow older some people start reading horror stories and watching more and more violent films; train for, and get involved with extreme sports. Even the horrors explicitly outlined of the outcome of drug taking, does not stop some people experimenting with them in order to reach a state of mind which they feel cannot be achieved in the state of 'normality'.

I also think that some people venture into Spiritualism looking for that unknown thrill which they have yet to experience. Their heads are full of the nonsense portrayed about spirit and Spiritualism in the media and literature and which they believe totally. I find it extremely strange that people do not question the authors and creators of such information. If I wish to study a new subject or be trained in a new discipline I will make sure that the person(s) who will teach me are fully qualified and further,

WHAT IS NOT SPIRITUALISM

will not accept what they tell me if it cannot be substantiated by facts and figures. I realise some things have to be accepted on trust, but such things will have to make sense to me or I will always have trouble with the theory put forward.

Once many are involved in Spiritualism and begin to understand a little more and are witness to the fact that there really is a spirit world wherein dwell many inhabitants, then the horrors, witnessed on film, or written in books, surface and they are looking over their shoulders convinced that demons, devils and other nasties are just waiting to pounce. It is also an unfortunate fact that Spiritualism itself, within its literature, and by discussion with Spiritualists, sometimes perpetuates these myths.

One of the most frequently asked questions is: "Are there evil spirits" and it really isn't possible to give a straightforward "Yes" or "No". This is due to fact that notwithstanding the fact that everyone has been given eternal life by that creative energy source which men call God, we are, in the main, our own masters and answer to ourselves for the lives we lead and how we interact with others during that life. It therefore follows that the definition of 'evil' made by the majority, does not hold true for every individual and everyone will define evil within their own understanding. I consider eating human flesh to be evil, but for a cannibal it was the greatest compliment which could be paid to you. Also, when the choice is either consume the carcass of a dead colleague or perish, then who am I to judge another's actions or motives.

We are all unique individuals and are at different stages on the evolutionary pathway of eternity and there are some people who I consider have a lot to answer for and while I do not know the motives for their actions and cannot sit in judgment upon such actions, I would still prefer never to be in their company. I do not need to list these people as I

The Cult!

Evangelistic Cult Assult

think we are all aware of some of those who have caused chaos in our world and/or hurt thousands of people. In my book this is practically unforgivable, but evidently not in theirs.

We are told by the more evolved spirit people, the teachers and the guides, that when we leave our physical bodies behind we are home; back in the world we left to journey to earth. They also tell us that because of the Law of Attraction, everybody will be with like-minded people which means we will be with those we love, our families, friends and our spirit guides and helpers. In fact we will be distanced from these people who actions have filled us with fear, dread and horror.

That is not to say that these people are abandoned because they are not. There are beautiful souls watching for a flicker of remorse or a tear shed for their deeds. Such signs are immediately acted upon and that soul will start working its way back into the light of its own spirit. It is said that the realms wherein these souls dwell are dimmed by the darkness of their deeds and it is hoped that the majority of us will be the inhabitants of brighter realms.

It must also be remembered that the physical world actually has no substance to those living in spirit and that once we leave our bodies behind, the fabric of our houses, the country and seaside, everything dissolves as we enter the spirit world which is a new dimension and wherein the houses and gardens are equally as substantial as those we left behind on earth, but are enhanced with a splendour which only spirit can give them.

When spirit are asked how they actually see those of us still living on earth, we are told they know us by our light and that the more spiritually aware we are, the brighter shines that light; their link to us is a mental one which is effected by the application of thought. So the scenario is: we are moving through our world as radiant light energy linked to the many hundreds of people in the spirit world who have a care for us and yet we fear these souls in the spirit world who presently abide in the darkness of their own ignorance, thoughts and actions? It really doesn't, and cannot, make sense!

So yes, there are people in the spirit world in need of extra care and attention by the more evolved spiritual beings who have charge over them, but

No, they can never have any effect upon any one of us - we are too far removed from them.

However, if you want to be spooked badly enough, I am sure your own imagination will oblige!

GHOSTS

There is such muddled thinking regarding ghosts, which are not spirit people, or people at all, just an impression of events or people, retained on the atmosphere of a place. I cannot think why any person would wish to walk the corridors of a castle where they once lived, throughout eternity. The fact that a ghostly impression of a person is being witnessed doing just this, has got to initiate the question, why?

The whole thrust of spirit teachings is that life is continuous, for everyone, not just the favoured few. When we leave our physical bodies behind we will find ourselves in the world of spirit. I am sure it does not look too different to earth at the level we will enter but it will slowly become obvious that we are no longer living on earth. Would my mind be so sick, even after being released from its body, to trap itself in a time warp in order to carry out the earthly duties for which I was once responsible? More questions, which must be asked, are: Would there not be any inhabitant of the spirit realms able to help me break free from such obsessive behaviour. Would my family be content to watch me behave in such a fashion without trying to obtain such help?

I feel we have the answer to ghosts in spirit teachings. We know that thought has a living energy and these ghostly impressions are formed by the thoughts of the people who carried out these repetitive tasks, over and over again in their earthly lives. These thoughts are embedded in the very fabric of the place where these actions took place and have been seen a sufficient number of times for the phenomenon to be recorded. Once recorded we then have to take into account the power of our own minds, which is immense and not yet fully understood. A suggestion placed into our minds that a 'white lady will be seen at 10 o'clock in the Ancestors Gallery, usually guarantees a number of sightings.

There are also audible ghosts as well as visionary ones and many places are haunted by the sounds of activities which took place on the haunted site. An old airfield in the South of England re-runs the 'scramble' when the siren goes and airmen are heard taking off in their planes and eventually returning. This has been repeated since the war years and continues right up until today but those airmen have returned home to spirit and are not still scrambling to save our shores.

It is possible for a spirit person to remain close to earth should they so desire and others may see such a person on occasion. That, however, does not make them ghosts; they are still people and will continue to be so. Mediums cannot communicate with ghosts; it would be like talking into the wind and expecting a reply.

We must educate the public into realising that while ghosts may traverse their timeless corridors, they are not part of Spiritualism, spirit teachings or Spiritualist philosophy.

GROUNDING

While grounding is not a serious problem within Spiritualism it is another expression which is being used a lot within the Movement and, to my mind, is totally unnecessary.

Grounding evidently is having to visualise your feet growing roots and having them immersed through the floor which will stop you flying away, I should imagine, but I am not too sure why this is considered necessary.

It is said that grounding is very, very necessary and the following is taken from www.mystic-mouse.co.uk website which tells us why it is important to ground ourselves:

"Grounding:
- Brings life in to matter and enables us to bring our healing abilities into the physical.
- Increases balance and stability in our physical and our emotional state.
- Helps bring acceptance that we are here to fulfil a purpose.
- Brings strength.
- Helps in creating a bridge between Spirit and matter.
- Provides an outlet making the release (of energy) easier.
- Allows the attainment of higher Spiritual levels.

As a healer it is very important to keep your patient grounded."

We are then told what can happen if we do not ground:
- Dizziness
- Daydreaming
- A feeling of being 'Spaced Out'
- Feeling sick

- Heart palpitations
- Eyes flickering
- Weight gain
- Clumsiness
- Static shocks
- Falling asleep when meditating
- Noise and light sensitive
- Forgetful
- Having brilliant ideas that never happen
- Arguing and unable to get your point across "

There is a note to the effect that it is possible that some of the above problems could be symptoms of a medical condition.

We are then given information on how to become more grounded:

- "Eating (hence sometimes the weight gain) - healthy and balanced.
- Drinking water
- Walking, especially in natural surroundings
- Sports, yoga, tai chi etc.
- Gardening
- Animals e.g. walking the dog
- Being purposeful
- Visualization of roots/colour
- Carrying/working with crystals"

The information concludes with the rooting visualisation; the colours for grounding: red, brown and terracotta. It also names the crystals we should carry about our person which can help, these being Red Jasper (evidently most Jaspers are good for grounding), Bloodstone, Hematite, gold Tigers Eye, Carnelian, Garnet, Pyrite, Copper, Amber, Unakite.

Unfortunately there is no advice given as to how those of us who work as healers should ground our patients.

I think the idea of the rooting visualisation is to ensure that you will not be prone to flights of fancy while working with spirit as you are solidly rooted. This supposition is silly as people prone to such flights of fancy will have them whether or not they visualise their feet encased in clay. I find the whole concept ridiculous and have never once grounded in all my 30 something years as a medium and, strangely enough, have never seriously suffered from any of the symptoms listed which are said to be caused by non-grounding.

I think what people are trying to get across is that it is very necessary for people to 'keep their feet on the ground' and remain well balanced as increasing sensitivity can make mediums temperamental and a little bit 'touchy' until they develop the ability to deal with it.

I can imagine being held up in traffic, arriving at the Church late, rushing onto the rostrum and saying "Can you wait while I open up all my chakras, ground myself, play with my crystals and ask for protection. When I have finished I will then be able to work."

We know spirit will be there with us, eager and ready to work without all this totally unnecessary mental ritual for that is all it is. Not only is it an unnecessary mental ritual it can cause confusion to a novice medium and may cause worry regarding health problems which they may now ascribe to be caused by non-grounding

It is known that some mediums do have problems after doing services. An altered state of consciousness is achieved in order for the mediums to connect with spirit and do their work. Sometimes that connection is so strong they have difficulty coming back to reality. Crystals will not help, neither will imagining roots for feet. Refreshments and a chat usually do the job.

LIGHT WORKERS AND EMPATHS

Over the years, mainly since the advent of the Internet, there appears to be a lot of new terminology entering the Spiritualist vocabulary, Light Workers and Empaths being two of them.

A light worker is someone who is not only an enlightened person but is also actively working within this enlightenment, i.e. as a medium, healer, or in any other spiritual capacity which is of service to mankind. As the name indicates, they are working with the light which term, quite frankly, doesn't really make sense to me but I am assuming it is used to show that they are not using any abilities they have for materialistic gain or for self-gratification or glory.

I am not sure why someone who works as a healer or a medium has to become part of the Light Workers group. We already know (see Evil Spirits section) that people in the Spirit World see us by the light of our individual spirits. It must follow, therefore, if we are already light, why would we want to call ourselves Light Workers? I am also of the opinion that the point of enlightenment takes place when a person realises that they are spirit and not just a material body. There are a lot of enlightened souls on our planet and not all of them are Spiritualists; some of the greatest souls who have ever lived were not Spiritualists but they were certainly very spiritual

I do think we have a tendency to put labels on everything and everyone but surely when we start putting labels on labels, then is the time to stop. It also seems to cause a lot of self complacency, reading between the lines, of some of the information given on the internet as to the definition of Light Workers; some practically see themselves as angels and I am afraid they are in danger of losing their light within their own adoration.

Another re-labelled word is psychic. Every person is psychic, to a greater or lesser degree; we all have our moments of intuition and of 'too many coincidences' to make us realise that there are times when we become aware of others' thoughts, emotions and pain. It is by developing our psychic ability that we can reach out with our minds and connect with the Spirit World and, with the help of our Spirit Guides, connect with Spirit.

Now we are being introduced to Empaths who are extremely sensitive to other people's thoughts, emotions and pain. Sounds very much like a Psychic to me. Evidently some Empaths are all heart and have difficulty at times in rationalising or thinking logically which seems a heavy price to pay for something which is natural and can be controlled. No one has to be linked into every person they meet, when they meet. Training within Spiritualism teaches us how to open and close our awareness and so protect ourselves for tuning in to others pains and emotions. I have been accused of being very unfeeling for wanting to disassociate from another's pain and I am not quite sure why I would want to feel them in the first place - same with the emotions. I cannot remove them; I can be sympathetic without actually feeling them so I am not sure what problem these so-called 'Empaths' have. Some claim living is so difficult because they are continually bombarded by everyone's emotions and they cannot leave the house at times. I also know that they do not like being told that they are just psychic the same as everyone else so again, we are coming up against the age-old phenomenon called ego.

All mediums and psychics are sensitives and the majority learn to control it and live with it.

Within Spiritualism there is quite a bit of new terminology newcomers have to learn without the addition of such unnecessary expressions as Light Workers and Empaths.

LOST SOULS

This is another area with which I cannot come to terms. Perhaps it is just the word 'lost' that causes such a stumbling block for me. I cannot conceive how anyone can be lost?

One of the first things that can occur in a development circle is that one of these 'lost souls' will attach itself to a novice medium and cause lots of tears and gnashings of teeth. The circle members will then gently talk to this lost soul and direct it towards the light. Everyone sits back, pats themselves on the back – another soul saved. I am not being facetious here, even though it may sound as though I am, I am simply relating what happens because I have been there, done it, and got the t-shirt. I have also been told by countless other people that this is one of the first things that happened when they sat in a circle.

I have questioned how this is possible, especially with a novice medium whose guides have not yet managed to influence the medium to the point of control and yet a wandering, 'lost soul' can; is this soul helped by the novice's guides to take control? I would hate to think that any of my guides would allow this to happen and I do know that many novice mediums have curtailed their mediumship development because of such experiences. It is possible, therefore, that Spiritualism has lost some beautiful mediums consequent upon these experiences.

We all have free will and there is nothing stopping us from choosing to remain close to earth after we have left our physical bodies, but that choice does not put us in the legions of lost souls.

I also have difficulty coming to terms with the theory that it is possible for any of us to ever become lost when we are all linked to the Godhead which is responsible for the creation and continuing evolvement of every single one of us.

It is known when every person is to return to spirit, even when the death is accidental or appears to be sudden, and there is always someone waiting to greet everyone. If some people choose to linger close to earth, then that is their choice but it is hard to conceive that they can be lost when there are so many great souls in spirit overseeing and caring for every person on earth.

It is possible that some Spirit people, when told that they have left their physical bodies and are now living in spirit may find this hard to believe and in fact choose not to believe it. However, surely the facts that their friends on earth are ignoring them; the walls of their homes, if they can see them at all, are semi-transparent and can be walked through and there are people they know to be dead who are talking to them, has got to make them sit down and wonder. They may feel they are dreaming and refuse any offers of help made to them. Eventually, however, they will become aware of the reality of their surroundings and perhaps find that the 'dream' is far more pleasant than was their life on earth.

We are told by spirit guides that the spirit world is home and that when we vacate our physical bodies we will be going home. Is it suggested that we will not recognise our home? Perhaps not immediately but I am certain that when our spirits are released from their physical restraints, memories of home will return and we will remember many things, especially our origin.

So what is happening in the circles, because these novice mediums are not doing this deliberately or play-acting?

If we check in some of the Spiritualists' National Union's educational courses we find the following which relates to trance mediumship:

"When a medium is passing into, or out of, a trance control, it is sometimes obvious that there is an intermediate state in which the medium's subconscious is in control. First the conscious self withdraws and gives place to the subconscious, which finally yields its place to the spirit control."

Could this not be the answer? The novice's subconscious is in control, and is perhaps unsure as to where it is and what is happening?

The difficulty with this supposition is that people find it difficult to accept any other hypothesis than that which they have already decided upon. Some have possibly read about lost souls and the thought of being able to help these people may well be embedded in their subconscious minds.

There will be other people who have no knowledge whatsoever of lost souls and yet will still not concede that they are capable of producing what I choose to call 'the lost soul phenomenon' themselves. They are adamant that there is a control outwith themselves and they are just facilitating an energy in order for it to be released.

I have always found that the most simple answers usually make the most sense and I can certainly accept that the number of occasions I was troubled and spoke 'as a lost soul' could be the production of my subconscious mind, clearing out its rubbish in order for my spirit guides to draw close and then exert their control.

As far as I am concerned, anyone who experiences this phenomenon should take comfort from the fact that it is quite possible that he or she has the potential for trance mediumship should they wish to pursue its unfoldment within a circle.

To quote Silver Birch yet again: "If your reason cannot accept it, then reject it."

ORBS

With the advent of digital cameras there appears to be an influx of photographs with orbs on them and strangely enough, not many people seem to notice the coincidence of this fact. People are actually getting very excited about what are, in fact, spoiled photographs. I have looked at hundreds of them, sent to me by such excited people claiming that the orbs are either elementals or spirit people. How can anyone reduce a person to an orb?

Firstly, with digital cameras, if the exposure/light setting is not quite right the camera will compensate by guessing what is being refracted through its lens. Secondly, and more commonly, there is often a slight delay between depressing the 'shoot' button and the flash working which is the most common reason for this phenomenon.

I hold photographs of what look like very tiny flying saucers and the producer of such snaps is convinced, because "a medium has told her", that she has captured elementals on film. A photographic expert advised that what she has actually done is capture insects in flight, which can be done with digital cameras. Our lady photographer became very incensed when told it was insects - she wanted it to be fairies, so fairies they are.

The Spiritualists' National Union holds hundreds of spirit photographs and on all of them the spirit people show themselves as people in order to be recognised. To impress a film with such an image, energy must be available and many of the more older pictures were produced by the spirit people using ectoplasm provided by the medium. There are also what I like to call 'spontaneous spirit photographs' where the sitters did not deliberately sit with a medium in order to facilitate a spirit extra. These spontaneous photographs are totally unexpected and it is not always obvious who supplied the energy but when the person is recognised, then it is obvious that there is a spirit agency involved and energy was found to produce the snap.

These photographs were taken in the early days of cameras and yet spirit managed to show themselves as the real people they are. How can it be suggested that in this age of technology in which we live, that they are now reduced to representing themselves as orbs? This does not make sense as we know that the spirit scientists are always one step ahead of us and it is highly likely that the concept of digital cameras came originally from spirit.

There are, however, photographs which have circles of light on them which are acknowledged as spirit lights. These spirit lights have been appearing in séance rooms since spirit first encouraged people to sit in circles.

Using today's technology, i.e. video equipment, spirit lights have been captured on film zig-zagging all around the room indicating that there is an intelligence creating such phenomenon.

It is important, therefore, that people learn to differentiate between spirit lights and orbs (particles of dust and/or moisture in the air). If it is considered that the orbs are created by spirit and are, in fact, spirit lights, then experimentation should immediately take place to try and establish the medium for such production thereby giving the spirit people the opportunity to expand on these lights and eventually create faces and forms.

Until then, please don't try and turn my Grandmother into an orb and until it can be proved to the contrary, let us keep orbs in the digitals and not in Spiritualism.

POSSESSION

Possession is said to be when a disembodied spirit, of no good intent, takes over control of your body; moves it through its daily locomotion and talks through it, usually spewing forth a lot of filth in the process. Sometimes the possession can be total and at other times, just partial.

Unfortunately there are so many people, inside and outside of Spiritualism, who actually think this can happen and in consequence are very fearful of our religion. The thought that perhaps by becoming involved in Spiritualism, and Mediumship, they could be placing their own bodies at risk has got to be a terrifying thought and I think the greatest fear of all is that these entities are just waiting for new bodies to control. It really does smack of Invasion of the Body Snatchers.

For a God, which is an energy of total and absolute love, to allow its spirit children (us) to be pushed out of our physical bodies by some discarnate nasty entities is actually laughable; it makes a nonsense of our understanding and conception of God and the meaning of Love.

If we study and/or experience Astral Projection, where the spirit, in its etheric vehicle, leaves the physical body it can be seen that the spirit body is always attached to the physical body by what is known as the Silver Cord. This seems to be a ray of energy, appearing as light, which can elongate to any length to allow the spirit to travel and which pulls the spirit back to its own body at the end of its journeyings. This, too, can appear to be science fantasy until it is actually experienced in a fully conscious condition. When that happens what it actually does is just confirm that the body is not the animating force and that the consciousness resides in the spirit. This, then, confirms all the spirit teachings and communications which Spiritualists receive.

In Spirit Teachings, if we have not already discovered it, we are told that there is a Law of Attraction; Like attracts Like and I fail to see, therefore, how anyone can ever be fearful of being influenced by a nasty piece of goods in the spirit world unless they, too, are also nasty. The person concerned would also have to be susceptible to spirit control and the spirit would have to be capable of exerting such control. Control is not necessarily possession; control is usually an influence exerted upon the medium, usually by his or her spirit guide and this can be done without even being near to the medium; it is mind control which is allowed by the medium.

It therefore follows then that the only people who could be influenced, outside of their will, or knowledge, are people who are not in control of their own minds. People with such huge mental problems are usually being helped in hospitals and the only kind of spirit I could envisage coming near such people are our Healing Guides and Helpers as they direct healing energy towards them. There would be no point in a spirit intent on doing harm coming close to such people because if they did and caused problems the patients would be subdued.

The problem of spirit possession is often confused with multiple personalities and confused mental states and people insist that they are possessed and I am certain this is not the case. There are too many things in life that we do not understand and one of them is the power of our own minds.

Possession is not possible but obsession is. The mind is a powerful tool and wrongly used can play tricks. If people have been told, or are themselves convinced, that they are possessed then the mind will oblige.

One point to consider when worrying about being possessed is the fact that some mediums sit for quite a long time waiting to be entranced (or influenced) by spirit and yet people who have not started their mediumistic development think they can be possessed - it cannot happen. To be entranced the spirit guides need to be involved to assist in the entrancement. Would someone's guides assist in a possession? As far as I am concerned, it cannot happen without them.

If there was as much danger as people think there is, then I am afraid there would be a lot fewer mediums working for spirit than there is. Not that mediums do not have courage, I hasten to add, but to work for spirit while under a vicious influence would be a little pointless and non productive.

I cannot, therefore, make sense of, or accept, spirit possession - obsession, yes! - possession, no!

PROTECTION

Unfortunately, this is another area in which I find I have huge problems and yet the majority of mediums ask for protection, usually in the opening prayer but they never say why there is a need for it. I often wonder if it is in deference to the statement in the Lords Prayer which asks "Lead us not into temptation and deliver us from evil."As far as I am concerned both temptation and evil are only states of mind and can differ according to the mind which is analysing them.

So, we ask for protection when holding a religious service which makes a nonsense of the fact that the service is a time in which to be at one with our God; to praise and venerate whatever we perceive our God to be. Do we need protection from God?

We sit in circle to work with our spirit helpers to unfold our mediumistic potential and we ask for protection. Are these helpers going to do us harm? Are they incapable of preventing unwanted spirit, perhaps of a mischievous nature, infiltrating our circles?

When checking the website http/www.mystic-mouse.co.uk we are told that our auras can be invaded by negative energies if we do not protect ourselves. Whilst I do not disagree with this statement I am always fully protected at all times because I will not allow myself, or my aura, to be invaded by such energies. As long as I am convinced that I am untouchable, I will remain so; it is a simple affirmation; a simple knowing that does not even have to be expressed. The only area where I have any concern is not discarnate spirit but spirit incarnate. Thoughts have a living energy and some people send out some nasty thoughts and novice mediums are advised to keep themselves closed off and keep positive in their thinking. The only problem with this is that surely closing off to negative energies is also closing off to positive energies.

Some people use the power of the mind, to visualise themselves surrounded by a mirror which reflects such thoughts back to the sender. I do not find this necessary as no one can touch me unless I allow them to and there is a universal law expressed in the sixth principle, Compensation and Retribution, which effectively means give out good and good will be returned; give out bad and bad will be returned, 1,000-fold. It is easier to allow the law to run its course.

There is then a list of the symptoms we may experience if we are open to psychic attack and they are:
- "Irritable/losing your temper
- Drained
- Nightmares
- Easily influenced by others
- Threatened/defensive
- Fanatical about someone
- Feeling other peoples emotions/pain
- Bumping into people

- Copying or living your life through others
- On a physical level you can feel pain in the back of your neck, solar plexus (pit of stomach), or wrists."

And the remedies to cure such symptoms are:
- "Keep fit and well
- Drink lots of water
- Wear protective colours - for example gold, silver, violet or blue
- Wear or carry crystals with a protective quality - for example Amethyst, Lapis Lazuli, Sugilite, Laramar, Gold Tigers Eye and Hawks Eye (blue tigers eye) for psychic protection.
- Wear or use protective symbols - for example The Egyptian Ankh, Rune symbol, Star of David (six pointed star), Circle, Egg, Pentagram (five pointed star, especially for Wiccans/Pagans), Pyramid or Cross. Symbols are very personal things, so only wear or carry what feels right for you and what you are comfortable with.

Visualization - for example a good exercise is to imagine you are sitting in an egg of light. The base of the egg is sitting just below the floor (so you are grounded) and you are surrounded in your egg by a lovely protective colour (gold, silver, violet or blue). You make sure that your eggshell is solid so that no negative energy can penetrate it.

Any negative thoughts/emotions that you may have will not get out and no negative thoughts/emotions from others will be allowed in. In turn each negative energy or thought pattern will hit the eggshell and slide down it into the ground to be transmuted in to positive energy."

So......... the question has to be asked. If it is necessary to be protected, who on earth are we trying to protect ourselves from?

I have found, to my cost, as I am sure many people have, that if others are determined to hurt you, then no amount of praying for protection will help, otherwise there would be no point in any of us having free will. Knowing that we are all immortal beings and that there are Spiritual Laws in place which will deal with all misdemeanours, including our own, should be sufficient to help us cope as we best we can when in difficult circumstances.

Having said all that, if on a personal level, you are more comfortable when asking for protection, then do so by all means. Never put any stress upon yourself and always do what feels right to you but, at the same time, do not put stress on others, like me, by insisting that I must think, and do, the same as you.

PSYCHIC WEBSITES

Thankfully the Age of the Internet is with us and we can access a mine of information by surfing its many pages. We can also access a mine of misinformation if we are ignorant of our subject matter or do not know who the authorities are and whether or not they can be trusted.

There are hundreds of sites, with and without chatrooms, available to instruct us. One chatroom personnel were discussing an incubus when I entered. I asked if this was the No. 56 to Kings Cross? Would you be surprised to learn that I was booted and banned from this site?

You may also be interested to know that all the evil spirits are alive and well and living on the Internet. The number of people who are authorities on evil spirits is quite incredible. Everyone has had an experience with one or more and register surprise when I confess that I have never met one or been bothered by one. I know that like attracts like and these spirits are with souls similar to themselves. I am certainly not similar to them and when I point this out can you guess who gets booted and banned?

To say visiting a psychic chatroom can be an eye-opener is putting it mildly.

Having said the above, however, there are some excellent sites which give me hope for the future but I am not too sure how a novice would know the difference.

There are mothers who come to these sites wanting to understand how mediumship works and whether or not it can help them. They sit and listen to people discussing lost souls who cannot find 'the light' and are wandering in a limbo of darkness. Some of these mothers, who have lost a child, are now watching the screens with dread in their hearts wondering if their little ones are wandering in this darkness. Some people should think before they speak and then perhaps not bother.

It is important, therefore, that everyone realises that the majority of these websites have no real bearing on Spiritualism whatsoever. On some, any information regarding Spiritualism has been copied (Silver Birch in particular). The Seven Principles of Spiritualism given to the Spiritualists' National Union by the spirit of Robert Owen, through the mediumship of Emma Hardinge Britten in 1871, can be seen on many of these sites. While the Spiritualists' National Union may or may not claim copyright and could be quite happy to share these Principles with the world, a simple acknowledgment would have been appreciated.

The Spiritualists' National Union has its own website, as does SNUi (Spiritualists' National Union International), and many of its Churches and all these sites are well worth a visit. When visiting spiritual or Spiritualist websites allow your commonsense to be your yardstick. Happy surfing!

REINCARNATION

Some people are of the opinion that reincarnation is theoretical, there not being sufficient evidence for it to be accepted as factual. Conversely others feel very strongly that the evidence recorded is substantial. This does not mean that it is not a fact and, conversely, it also does not mean that it is a fact. Strangely enough spirit guides differ when questioned upon the subject. Some say yes; some say no; some say yes in certain cases. People must, therefore, decide for themselves whether or not returning to earth to have more experiences makes sense.

As far as Spiritualism is concerned, Reincarnation cannot be part of its philosophy. Spiritualism is factually based; the teachings we propound tell of eternal existence while the communications received from our family and friends in the spirit world, which give evidence of their survival, support such teachings. There is insufficient evidence to support the theory of reincarnation - as far as SNU Spiritualism is concerned.

Because Spiritualists have freedom of thought and personal responsibility, many do believe in Reincarnation and while it is not put forward as part of Spiritualist teachings then people are at liberty to believe what they will.

My personal problem with Reincarnation is twofold:

1. It is claimed the Earth is the teaching/training ground for spirit and it is only by living a physical life, and re-living it until we get it right, that we can spiritually progress.

My question is: "What happens when the Sun goes nova?"

This is going to happen; it is a fact which cannot be ignored so at what point will people start being born on another suitable planet and is there another suitable planet? The solar system is vast while the Universe is even vaster and even though mankind may conquer space travel in order for him to colonise space, I have never read or heard of this event being put forward by spirit teachers when discussing the future of mankind.

2. It is also claimed that we cannot have all experiences in one lifetime and that is why we need to keep coming back in order to do this.

My question is: "What if there is only one experience required and that experience is 'living as spirit in a physical body in a material environment'?"

Only one experience of this nature is therefore required. There are so many intellectual, mental, emotional experiences which can take place on other planes of existence I do not understand why people get so bogged down with the need to have 'every' experience. We have eternity in which to do this, if this is what is required. I actually doubt this very much as there would not be much point in God creating us as unique individuals if we were all then expected to have the same, or similar, experiences; it smacks of cloning and God doesn't need to clone. It is said there are many pathways leading to God and I think this is a truth but it wouldn't make sense if we all had to walk the same pathway.

To cover all bases, I am sure that if there is a need for someone in the spirit world to incarnate once again upon earth, for a special reason, then it can, and will, happen. I can never limit spirit.

In conclusion may I remind people that the Seventh Principle of Spiritualism, given to us by Robert Owen through the mediumship of Emma Hardinge-Britten in 1871, is 'Eternal Progress open to every human soul who wills to tread the path of good'. - Progression - no mention of retrogression! It was also Emma, when asked the eternal question regarding reincarnation, replied: 'Does the eagle go back to the egg?'

RESCUE CIRCLES

Rescue Circles are set up by many Mediums in order to work with spirit to assist those people dwelling in the darkened spheres to be brought into the light. In many instances the 'evil' one is allowed to control the medium and is literally dragged screaming, shouting and swearing into the séance room. Once there the other Members of the circle will talk to this unfortunate soul and set him/her onto the path of righteousness once again. There are also many books written about the work of Rescue Circles but that fact does not make it any easier for me to understand them.

The main problem I have is that we are told that when we pass into spirit we progress, or regress, to the sphere most suited to us, taking into account the way we have conducted ourselves while living on earth. In this sphere, or level, we are with people of like mind, people similar to ourselves. If this is so then the people who have not acquitted themselves well while living out their earthly span are all together in some place suited to the darkness of their ignorance and gross deeds perpetrated upon others. It is then said that these spheres become a little brighter the more spiritually enlightened we become.

I have no problem with these levels of existence, we build our home in spirit by our thoughts, words and deeds on earth; I can accept that. What I cannot accept is that people from these lower levels can be brought through the intervening layers and then be shown how to control a medium whose spiritual light would, I suspect, blind such a soul. The fact of the matter is that we still have personal responsibility even when we have left this body and are in spirit and so do these souls. Also, we are told that people cannot be helped until they are ready for such help. Therefore, if a soul is ready for help why is he or she brought kicking, screaming and swearing into the Circle. That is illogical.

Again, I have to ask, where are the enlightened souls in spirit? Do they go on vacation when a spirit from the lower levels truly wishes to make reparation for everything he or she has done? Of course they don't! They are there, waiting, listening, watching for that tiny spark of light which will indicate that one soul is now ready to listen to reason and to acknowledge his/her mistakes.

Are we then to accept that these great souls, who can manage to cloak their lights and lower their vibrations in order to enter these levels, now need to bring them back to earth for someone to tell them to 'look for the light;?

I feel that in Spiritualism we have too many knights in shining armour looking for crusades.

So what is happening? The work of these circles continue and some spirit, or force, is still controlling mediums and being helped along its spiritual pathway. After a great deal of thought, and discussion with friends, I believe that what we have are mischievous people, who do not change when passing into spirit, who are continuing to play their games. Some people play such powerful, manipulative games while on earth and there is nothing, or no-one, to stop them still playing - just a change of venue!

What is of tremendous concern, however, is that people just coming into Spiritualism hear of these 'evil' spirits, have read the books and seen the films and can be so frightened of Spiritualism before they have really begun to investigate it. I do not believe there are as many 'evil' spirits as people are led to believe. The majority of people, even the misguided and mischievous ones, are basically good.

If it were possible for mediums to be attacked by such beings, then there would be no mediums working. The fact is, mediums develop their awareness to such a degree that they are aware of negative energies surrounding people and places.

It must be said, however, that there may very well be times when spirit do bring souls from lower levels into our circles - using the circles as stepping stones for the soul to adjust from one vibration to another. If this is to happen, the circle will normally be told what is to take place and its permission will be sought. Should such an event occur, this would not mean that the group had become a Rescue Circle - just another co-operative effort between the two worlds.

Quite often negative energies are ascribed to evil spirits which is not necessarily true. It's time we got sensible about spirit, spirit communication and the spirit world.

SHADOW PEOPLE

"Have you ever noticed a shadow-like figure race across the room seen only out of the corner of your eye, but gone when you turn your full vision in that direction?

Chances are you have and at the time you just disregarded it and went on about your business. However, stop and think about it for a minute. You will probably realize that you haven't only seen this phenomena once, but many, many times, just like millions of other people.

A growing number of people no longer believe that this is just a figment of their imagination and there is indeed a name for this phenomenon - Shadow People.

So what are "Shadow People?" Are they ghosts, visuals from another dimension, something from the demon realm, or none of the above?

Shadow People have been witnessed in many different shapes and sizes and are often described as lurking within a shadow. At times, they are perceived as full people, though their details may seem very different from humans. Many reports describe them as being thin figures ranging from just a few feet tall to up to 6 or 7 feet in height. In all cases, they appear for only a moment and then quickly disappear. This type of supernatural event is quickly becoming one of the most commonly reported apparitions, though no one is sure exactly what it is that they are seeing.

One theory is that the Shadow People are actually spirits whose energy is denser than what we usually encounter as far as apparitions are concerned. This suggests that they are essentially the same as a spiritual orb or vortex, just more dense than most. Photographic evidence indicates that orbs and vortexes with enough density can and do cast shadows, and though we apparently cannot see a Shadow Person itself with the naked eye, it is a dense enough entity that we can also see the shadow it casts.

So now we circle back to the original question - what exactly are Shadow People?. Please feel free to share with us any photos or stories you would like to share so that together we can solve this fascinating mystery!"[1]

It seems that many people think that there is a race of humans, apart from those living in the physical and spirit

---

[1] www.portalinspirations.com

worlds. These are the shadow people - are humanoid in appearance and yet we, in the physical world, can only see them as shadows.

These shadow people can often be seen out of the corner of the eye as they move around our world. I am not sure whether these people are considered to be an alien life form or the spirits of another race of humans who do not have the same physical molecular structure as we do.

What I do know, and am very certain of, is that if there was such a race of people then our spirit guides would have given us some indication of their existence, especially in view of the fact that some people claim to be able to see them.

There are no such people!

For us to see something out of the corner of our eyes means that we are aware of, or have seen, something physical. For anything to cast a shadow means there must be a solid object or person to cast a shadow. We really seem to be entering the world of J M Barrie where shadows have a mind of their own.

We all have had the experience of being aware of something, or somebody, out of the corners of our eyes but as our eyes are physical then what we are perceiving must also be physical. To be aware of people who live in the spirit world we enter an altered state of awareness in order to link to the spirit world and receive the images and sounds they are projecting to us. We do not, and cannot, use our physical eyes. The only time these can be used to see spirit is if we are sitters in a physical séance and spirit are manifesting themselves, or part of themselves, using ectoplasm taken from the gross matter of the body of a physical medium.

An insect flies past, car lights from two or three streets away flash past our vision - so quickly - gone before they can be registered. These flashes of perception can be so many things in the physical world but because we want them to be supernatural, we will settle for nothing less.

If you are seeing shadows which you are convinced have a non-physical origin, then invite other people to witness them with you. A fresh perspective can shed some light on the origin of the shadows.

If, after extensive investigation, coupled with factual testimony from witnesses, you are still convinced of the existence of shadow people, then submit your evidence for such to the Society for Psychical Research for that is where such things belong - certainly not within Spiritualism.

Mediums do not communicate with animals!

Mediums do not communicate with the Dead!

Mediums do not communicate with shadows!

Mediums communicate with people!

SHAPE-SHIFTERS

It is possible to purchase many books on shape-shifters, the majority of which are written as fact, rather than fantasy. It is claimed by one well-known author that he was told by a member of British Intelligence that the Royal family are shape-shifting reptilians.

One theory is that our planet is ruled by a group of people called the Illuminate who originally emigrated here from Mars. They are non-humans and therefore take on human form so as to run our planet undetected. These people occupy places of great authority in all the major countries of the world and basically, control our destiny. If there are too many of us they will use the cloak of terrorism to arrange for some of us to be wiped out; small nuclear devices, chemicals, wars are evidently all organised by these people to keep the flocks they tend at a manageable size.

Following on from the above, there is one question which needs to be answered and that is: are the people we communicate with in the spirit world men or reptiles? Also, are we to believe that our parents and spirit guides would not give us some indication that we are being ruled by such creatures if it were true. We have received so much guidance and information from spirit over the years that not to be given a tiny insight into such an important fact would be reprehensible of our friends in spirit.

A visit to: www.youtube.com/watch?v=ksPtnQmq2dc will show a video claiming to show evidence of these reptiles and who some of them are. It shows a few American Presidents and, interestingly enough, other important American people. The video is concentrated on their eyes and moves in closer, then retreats a little, moves back in and plays about in this manner for a while; changes colour of the faces and it is obvious that whoever is making this video is trying to draw our attention to the eyes of these people. Eventually the pupils of the eyes turn into slits, proving without a shadow of doubt that these people are reptiles. (I always had my suspicions about George Bush and Bill Clinton). These reptiles are followed by photographs of honest, upstanding people and their pupils, would you believe are round.

If the video wasn't so offensive it would be hilarious. I wonder if Bill Clinton and George Bush worked with people who themselves had eye problems. To believe that family, friends and colleagues would not have noticed that these people have reptile eyes is an insult to everyone who views this video. It is very odd that with the good guys, we only get one or two straight shots; no zooming in and out and no computer produced enhancements for, as far as I am concerned, that is what I was looking at.

A study of any of the books written using information received from Spirit Guides will show that they all agree on the fact that Man is the highest form of life and the concept of being managed like herds of farm animals by some shape-shifting reptilians is something which could not happen. I do not know that the Law of Physics could conceive of a manner in which a creature from another planet, and possibly, dimension, could de-materialise from one form and re-materialise in another. It is possible that the ability to do this is there and man has just not discovered it yet.

The spirit people need ectoplasm, taken from the body of a physical medium, in order to create the phenomenon of materialisation and this materialised form cannot be held for very long as the ectoplasm must be returned to the medium. For a reptile to change shape into a human and remain such is really going into the realms of the fantastic and yet so many people do believe this to be true.

I am of the opinion that this kind of thinking is used to explain the reason why some people are so manipulative, cruel, domineering, tyrannical etc. It evidently is not possibly for a member of the human race to behave in such a fashion, therefore that person cannot be a man/woman and must be a creature from outer space. I really feel the energy I am expending on this particular section is just energy thrown away and a complete waste of time.

I would just like to refer the reader to the following two quotes from Emma Hardinge-Britten in her book, Extemporaneous Addresses:

"Hence, while every animal is perfect in its degree, it is not perfect in relation to the highest of forms, which is man."
"... whilst the spirit of man, as the perfect elaboration of form, the elaboration of intellect, the

cosmos that binds up all of existence known or conceived of in the universal mind - this remains forever. The imperfect dies; the beautiful and perfect, never."

People are at liberty to believe anything that appeals to their senses. Unfortunately Spiritualism is in danger of becoming included in this kind of science fantasy.

TV MEDIUMS

It would be thought that having mediums invited to work on the TV, demonstrating the truths of spirit, would be something which should be welcomed. Unfortunately this is not always the case. The reason for this being that the mediums are not vetted and it appears that the TV company certainly has no one within its ranks qualified in this respect. I would suggest that it is not in its interests to be seeking the educated, experienced mediums as that may remove mediumship from under the umbrella of entertainment.

Having said that, there are some excellent mediums working on our behalf through the medium of TV but I feel that probably came about more by good luck than good management. So not all is lost.

If we look at what happens on a TV programme investigating Spiritualism and/or mediumship, the medium is not only expected to link with spirit, in horrendous conditions, but also be able to answer questions and basically teach Spiritualism and not all are qualified or capable of doing this. Every time a 'TV Medium' gets it wrong it reflects back on all of us.

To make an obvious point. If a TV company wishes to make a programme about a Christian Church Service, or any other religion's service, they will take their cameras and record one. If it is a discussion, a group of the religious order will be brought together and filmed in a studio. As a Spiritualist I have never yet been invited to join such a discussion group in order to pull their religion to pieces. Every time there is a discussion on Spiritualism and mediumship, however, representatives from other belief systems are always invited to attend and proceed to tear into Spiritualism and, by so doing, make a mockery of their own spiritual beliefs. As a Spiritualist I would refuse to take part in a 'free for all' on another person's religion; my understanding being that we are all unique individuals with different needs, including our religious pathways.

Why then are we, as Spiritualists, allowing our mediums to be chewed up and spit back out like wet rags in the name of entertainment?

Perhaps it is 'pie in the sky' but it would be interesting, as well as beneficial to Spiritualists, if all TV mediums had a meeting and drew up a code of practice on the manner in which they will co-operate with the TV Moguls. Until that day comes we must be prepared to keep protesting when we see 'Psychic Programmes' which not only have lost the plot but also does not reflect the religion of Spiritualism.

VORTICES

"According to Pete A. Sanders Jr. and Richard Dannelley in their works Scientific Vortex Information and Sedona Power Spot Vortex respectively, vortexes are labelled according to the direction of their energy flow. Up-flow Vortexes, where energy is flowing upward out of the earth; and Inflow Vortexes, where energy is flowing inward, toward the earth.

Up-flow Vortexes are said to boost spiritual skills associated with going to a higher level. They are said to stretch or expand consciousness, like filling a balloon with air. Places labelled as a magnetic vortex are areas of inflow energy. An area labelled an electric vortex is an area of up-flow energy.

While an experience at an Up-flow Vortex is exhilarating, an inflow area generates a much more pensive feeling. Because the power of the vortex is flowing down rather than up, the energy at an inflow site feels heavier. On a spiritual quest or during introspective exploration, if not prepared, the first things people experience is Fear. As a result inflow areas are often thought of as negative or evil."[1]

"Thus said, Vortexes are areas of high energy concentrations, originating from magnetic, spiritual, or sometimes unknown sources. Additionally they are considered to be gateways or portals to other realms, both spiritual and dimensional. Vortexes typically exist where there are strong concentrations of gravitational anomalies, in turn creating an environment that can defy gravity, bend light, scare animals, twist plant life into contorted shapes, and cause humans to feel strange. Many vortexes have been shown to be associated with Ley Lines and have been found to be extremely strong at node points where the lines cross. Worldwide, the Great Pyramid in Egypt and Stonehenge in England are perhaps the most well known as centres of vortex activity, lesser known the God and Magog Hills. Often overlooked, not known, or discounted as vortex influences, but equally as powerful and fully interrelated in the overall scheme of things, are Personal Body Vortexes and solar or Sun Vortexes, discussed as well further on."[2]

---

[1] www.earthdragon.moonfruit.com/#/vortexes/4519719992
[2] www.Angelfire.com

"A vortex (plural: vortices) is a spinning, often turbulent, flow of fluid. Any spiral motion with closed streamlines is vortex flow. The motion of the fluid swirling rapidly around a centre is called a vortex. The speed and rate of rotation of the fluid are greatest at the centre, and decrease progressively with distance from the centre.

The fluid pressure in a vortex is lowest in the centre where the speed is greatest, and rises progressively with distance from the centre. This is in accordance with Bernoulli's Principle. The core of a vortex in air is sometimes visible because of a plume of water vapour caused by condensation in the low pressure of the core. The spout of a tornado is a classic and frightening example of the visible core of a vortex. A dust devil is also the core of a vortex, made visible by the dust drawn upwards by the turbulent flow of air from ground level into the low pressure core.

The core of every vortex can be considered to contain a vortex line, and every particle in the vortex can be considered to be circulating around the vortex line. Vortex lines can start and end at the boundary of the fluid or form closed loops. They cannot start or end in the fluid. (See Helmholtz's theorems) Vortices readily deflect and attach themselves to a solid surface. For example, a vortex usually forms ahead of the propeller disk or jet engine of a slow-moving airplane. One end of the vortex line is attached to the propeller disk or jet engine, but when the airplane is taxiing the other end of the vortex line readily attaches itself to the ground rather than end in midair. The vortex can suck water and small stones into the core and then into the propeller disk or jet engine.

Two or more vortices that are approximately parallel and circulating in the same direction will quickly merge to form a single vortex. The circulation of the merged vortex will equal the sum of the circulations of the constituent vortices. For example, a sheet of small vortices flows from the trailing edge of the wing or propeller of an airplane when the wing is developing lift or the propeller is developing thrust. In less than one wing chord downstream of the trailing edge of the wing these small vortices merge to form a single vortex. If viewed from the tail of the airplane, looking forward in the direction of flight, there is one wingtip vortex trailing from the left-hand wing and circulating clockwise, and another wingtip vortex trailing from the right-hand wing and circulating anti-clockwise. The result is a region of downwash behind the wing, between the pair of wingtip vortices. These two wintip vortices do not merge because they are circulating in opposite directions.

Vortices contain a lot of energy in the circular motion of the fluid. In an ideal fluid this energy can never be dissipated and the vortex would persist forever. However, real fluids exhibit viscosity and this dissipates energy very slowly from the core of the vortex. (See Rankine vortex). It is only through dissipation of a vortex due to viscosity that a vortex line can end in the fluid, rather than at the boundary of the fluid. For example, the wingtip vortices from an airplane dissipate slowly and linger in the atmosphere long after the airplane has passed. This is a hazard to other aircraft and is known as wake turbulence."[1]

---

[1] www.wikipedia.com

It can be seen from an examination of the dictionary definition of vortices that they are natural earth phenomena which to my mind, like many other such phenomena, have been made out to be psychic or have some psychic energy or power. "Up-flow Vortexes are said to boost spiritual skills associated with going to a higher level." (Sanders and Dannelley). I am not sure that I understand or believe this. If it was that simple, then we would be all out chasing vortices in order to enhance our psychic and spiritual skills. I would not have thought it was possible to go to 'a higher level' until you had earned that level. That would be like asking a 5 yr old to cook a meal; not only silly but downright dangerous.

PORTALS

"Portal primarily refers to:

1. Portal (architecture) a gate, door, or tunnel.
2. Portal (fiction) a magical or technological doorway that connects two different locations in time or space.

A common device in science fiction is a portal, or stargate, allowing rapid travel between distant locations, often originating either as a natural phenomenon or technological device. It usually consists of two or more gateways, with an object entering one gateway leaving via the other instantaneously. An advantage of portal technology over a faster-than-light drive is that it can be imagined to work instantly, and optionally to travel to the past or future, or to alternate universes.

Although the portal is currently science fiction, the concept of wormholes is very similar, and may indeed permit instantaneous effective faster-than-light travel in the future."[1]

Among many people who work as psychics and mediums, there seems to be a lot of talk about spirits needing portals to contact our world or gain entrance to it. It was also printed in the world press that the mediums who visited the site of the Tsunami in 2004 claimed that this natural phenomenon had created a portal into the spirit world and that all the nasty spirits were going to use it to come into our world. I am not too certain why they would want to do that, considering we are on different vibrational and molecular structural levels, we would pass like ships in the night. There is a group in the UK who were allegedly told by spirit that by holding a spirit circle, or séance, they too had opened up, or were in danger of opening up, a portal between the two worlds. And again, only the nasties would use it. I wonder where the goodies go when these things happen?

Vortices are natural phenomena and inter-world portals are straight out of the pages of science fiction. Anyone looking for a portal within Spiritualism will probably be directed to the local Spiritualist Church door.

WALK-INS

Walk-ins, I feel, is an extremely strange theory which naturally purports to be fact. The purpose of walk-ins is very spiritual and I feel it is intended that this fact alone will make it acceptable.

Basically, Walk-ins are people from spirit who come back to Earth to help mankind. A person living on earth agrees to give up his body in order for one of these great souls to 'walk in' and take over his life, his family, his job,

---

[1] Wikipedia.com

his friends etc. By taking over an adult body means this evolved soul does not need to go through childhood, schooling etc. - a short cut to reincarnation?

The person who has given up his body, before his natural time on earth is over, is treated like a King in spirit for his great sacrifice, thereby assisting his own soul's progression. The general consensus of opinion relayed to us by spirit guides, that we plan our lives prior to taking on a physical body, appears to have been overlooked

The Walk-in now lives his body's original owner's life but because of his own beautiful nature, everyone starts to see a change in this person; he is more gentle, more neighbourly, more spiritual than he ever was before. Once the change is perfected and everyone gets used to the 'new' person, he can then set about changing the world.

In 1980 Ruth Montgomery, a noted writer of mysticism, brought out a book called 'Strangers Among Us' which states on its dust jacket:

"Strangers Among Us is an invaluable guidebook to help us pass through the troubled era ahead. For we must now enter a time of trial, the last two decades of the twentieth century, leading up to the shift of the earth on its axis at the century's end - a cataclysm long predicted by the psychic community and ushering in the New Age that will then dawn.

As if in answer to Man's most pressing needs at this crucial moment in the evolution of the cosmos, the author claims to have been alerted to the presence here on earth of Walk-ins, enlightened beings now secretly and anonymously among us, who will be our guides and spiritual mentors through the turbulent years to come."

The book claims all the information is given from a Group Soul in the spirit world and lists the catastrophes which are due to occur as the earth wobbles on its axis at the emergence of the new millennium.

These statements really do not make sense and as far as I am concerned, there are two reasons for this:

The earth was not going to wobble on its axis just because we entered a new millennium because we do not actually know how old the earth really is and whether we are now living at the start of a new millennium is arguable; the earth was around and evolving a long, long time before man started counting years or calculating geological ages; and:

I spoke to a Geology Professor in the 1980s about this wobble and all the calamitous events which were to subsequently occur and he just laughed; he told me that the earth is always wobbling on its axis and will continue to do so irrespective of any omens or portents.

In the event, there have been some catastrophes which happened at the start of the new millennium but unfortunately these have always occurred; there have not been any of the horrors predicted in this book. It is said in this book that it is as though the earth is going to give itself a great big shake and get rid of many undesirables such as "those who were sickly and had relied on pill-popping instead of their inner reserves, as well as most of the freeloaders, the thieves, and the greedy." I am sure the disabled will be very happy to read such comments. It appears that the Group Soul communicating with Ruth Montgomery is predicting a new world which will be a veritable Utopia with only the good, the strong, the healthy and spiritually minded living on it.

What I would like to know is: 'Who decides who stays and who gets thrown away?' Every person believes that what they do is right and that they are beautiful souls; no one is going to admit that they are greedy, freeloaders, thieves etc. The majority of people believe in themselves and can see faults in others but, unfortunately, not always in themselves.

While purporting to be a spiritually uplifting book with these enlightened souls' only purpose being to save mankind from itself, it actually cuts across all spirit teachings often making them look ridiculous. Someone, somewhere, seems to be forgetting that our earthly lives are only a very tiny drop in the ocean of eternity and throwing off the dross from earth will not bring about 'peace in our time.' Peace doesn't happen like that and, for that matter, may never happen on earth which, at the moment, is only one small part of the soul's journey. To my way of thinking there are too many variances in the level of each person's spiritual understanding and progression for there ever to be complete peace.

While the shape-shifters are said to come with evil intent, the Walk-ins are the saviours of the world. I really don't think we need either of them. Walk-ins have never been part of Spiritualist Philosophy and to my mind, never will be - they, too, are straight out of Science Fantasy

WHAT IS NOT SPIRIT

One last area to look at which is sorely in need of attention is using spirit to explain anomalies, coincidences, unexplained events etc. Anything which is not immediately identifiable is so often laid at the door of spirit, especially by newcomers to Spiritualism. They are also usually the people who are trying to tell the world of the new truths they have discovered and then leave themselves wide open to ridicule by not being analytical enough in the investigation of spirit and Spiritualism.

Much on the list you will recognise as they may have caused you concern, especially when alone in the house at the dead of night before you have then realised what is causing the phenomenon.

HOUSEHOLD PHENOMENA

Radiators and water cisterns banging, floors creaking, furniture settling etc. All these noise are natural noises usually attributable to a change in the temperature of the house - pipes contract and expand, central heating and other plumbing usually gurgles quite a lot and every house's floorboards have a good creak when the house settles for the night.

I once stood in the kitchen and watched the tap in the sink slowly turn itself on, there was an icy breeze down my right-hand side and the hairs on my neck stood on end. I was alone and a little bit scared. I discovered the pantry door was open and a cold draught was blowing on the right side of my body, the tap was broken and I suspect it may have been fear causing the hairs on the back of my neck to stand to attention.

A circle phenomenon which can, and often does, happen outside of circle and is often unfairly attributed to spirit intervention is Telekinesis - the movement of objects. Every object which has moved and which should not have done so is spirit once again trying to attract our attention, or more particularly spirit children playing with our ornaments and knick-knacks. This is not necessarily the case. Traffic outside the house, especially the larger vehicles, cause vibrations which can gradually move objects. We must also not discount our own mind power. There is no point in telling the world that thought has a living energy and then discounting our own power of thought because we want to believe that spirit moved it. There is also one other possible cause to be taken into account and that is poor memory. So let's rule out every other possibility before laying the blame, once again, at the door of spirit.

Again, I am not sure what the point of such movement would be, unless, in the case of a very elderly lady whom I watched receive a message in Church, it was to let her know that her husband who had just passed was still alive. This did have a beneficial effect on this lady's life so I do know that spirit will use such methods, as required, but not everything that is moved is due to them.

Doors opening, televisions turning themselves on can all have a very simple mechanical explanation and I cannot really see why spirit would waste energy doing such things. Even if it is only to attract our attention, as is often alleged, what next? They have our attention what are they going to do for their next trick? Unless we are mediums we cannot attune to them and learn what they wish to impart and they have already used all available physical energy to attract our attention. I have always found spirit to be a bit more subtle. If they want to get a message across to me and I ignore the urge to go to Church, then I usually meet someone who will interest me in whatever spirit want me to look at. There is a limit to how much spirit can interfere in our lives in any event;

they can guide us and sometimes advise us but they must not meddle anymore than we should meddle in anyone else's life.

OPTICAL PHENOMENA

Often when watching a medium working on the rostrum it is possible to see a white light all around them and many people think they are seeing the aura You will find if the medium moves and you don't move your head there is still a white light directly in front of you. A lot of mediums don't see auras so how can people who have not developed their sensitivity to any degree be able to see what is claimed to be the physical aura just by staring. It is an optical illusion. If the white outline remains around the medium when s/he moves then it is possible that the more physical part of the aura is being seen.

There is a tendency, not done deliberately, to frighten ourselves quite a lot; usually caused by fear of the unknown. I was once asked to sit in a physical séance as members of the circle were complaining about seeing dark shadows in two corners of the room. This was happening every week; nearly the whole circle were seeing them and it was beginning to worry them. I sat and took note, tried not to giggle and waited until we had left the séance room and were having refreshments before I told them what the problem was, together with its solution.

The circle room was dimly lit and there was a medium put into the cabinet each week and the group concentrated on him, giving their energies to his guides to help with the development of his mediumship. As I sat I also concentrated on him, noticing that he was wearing a white shirt and one or two ladies in the group were also wearing white tops. It is a well known fact that if you stare long enough at a red spot and then transfer your eyes and look elsewhere you will then see a green spot. This is what was happening in the circle. Everyone was staring at the medium's white shirt and when they moved their eyes for a moment, there were black shadows in the corners, either side of the cabinet.

CIRCLE PHENOMENON

Another error in the séance room are all the Eskimo guides. I think I have been given a whole village of them, over the years. Every time I mentioned I was frozen in the circle, I was given an Eskimo guide. I could never understand this as I don't relate Eskimos to coldness; they may live in a land of ice and snow but they are so wrapped up in furs, they must be beautifully warm. Also, I do not think guides bring with them the physical conditions in which they lived when on earth, we usually sense their personality and the warmth of their love and compassion.

As I continued with my studies while sitting in circle I came to realise that it was a loss of energy causing the lowered temperature and all my Eskimo Guides are now refreshed after circle with a cup of coffee.

MENTAL PHENOMENON

There is also the phenomenon of seeing faces in front of closed eyelids just before dropping off to sleep. So many people are convinced that they are seeing spirit faces and never think to question why they only see them when in that totally relaxed state prior to sleep. They sit in circle and relax but do not see unidentified spirit faces, for it is very rare that any of these faces are recognised - at least I have never recognised any when I have witnessed them. They do not respond if you send a thought to them and there is no reaction to your presence whatsoever. This is understandable as this phenomenon is well known to Psychologists as the Hypnagogic Image which is an image(s) experienced by a person just before falling asleep, which often resembles a hallucination

It is actually a term coined by Alfred Maury for the transitional state between wakefulness and sleep.

While we have the Hypnagogic state, just prior to sleep when we see faces, there is also what is known as the Hypnopompic state, which is exactly the same state but takes place as we are beginning to awaken.

There is also a state similar to the Hypnagogic state which does not appear to have a name but which relates to sound rather than imagery.

TRAFFIC ANGELS

It appears that quite a number of Spiritualist drivers have access to spirit parking attendants and that whenever they wish to find a parking space, a thought goes out to spirit and the space is provided. That certainly increases the number of jobs awaiting us when we go home to spirit; apart from taking up an apprenticeship as an electrician in order to mess with the electrics, we can also become parking space providers for those still living on earth. WOW!

Looking at the logistics of a scenario we would first have to assume that spirit have nothing better to do in the spirit world but sit around waiting for us to call upon them to avail ourselves of their services. This certainly is not the case and I know I shall be busier when I am in spirit than I have ever been here but as I will be doing work that inspires and motivates me, then I am sure I will be pursuing my own spiritual evolvement at the same time. But I will certainly be busy; whether or not you are is your personal choice.

I receive a frantic message that a car parking space is needed so I jump into my uniform and check out the position. Using the train of thought being sent out to me, I can establish where my driver is. I would then need to link into the thoughts of all the other car drivers in the car park to check who was ready to leave, thereby creating a vacant space for my driver. Once that is established I would then have to influence my driver and direct him or her to the required space. This is where I foresee a difficulty. The driver could be harassed, running late, have battling schoolchildren in the car and generally, not really open to spirit influence. Many mediums, who are experienced recipients of spirit communications, would have difficulty receiving in such conditions. Some people who claim to receive such assistance are unable to give a very brief message in an Open Circle because of the lack of their mediumship development but when they need a parking space, they seem to receive loud and clear.

I do know that it often appears as though spirit are working for us when everything goes right, the traffic lights are all on green and we can always find a space when we need one but, in my opinion, this really is just coincidence and we should be thankful for it. I know that any requests for assistance of this nature I may receive when I am in spirit will be ignored. I do know that spirit encourage us to ask for their help when we are in need but I really think we have to give some serious consideration how great a parking space need is.

CHURCH/MEDIUMSHIP PHENOMENON

It will be found that the majority, if not all, of the Psychic-Mediumistic-Spiritual websites on the Internet claim that everything that happens thereon is for Entertainment Purposes only and under 18 year old people are discouraged from using these sites. This is in order for them to stay within the Law.

Notwithstanding this Spiritualism is not an entertainment, it is a Science, a Philosophy and a Religion, and will never class itself as entertainment. Entertaining it can be but entertainment, never! It is also not Vaudeville and yet I have often sat in a service, as a member of the congregation and witnessed what can only be described as pure Vaudeville, with all its dirty innuendo and slapstick. What is even worse, and more to our shame, is the fact that the congregation were in fits of laughter and encouraging the medium to be more and more adventurous as to the depths he was prepared to plumb to elicit such raucous and disgraceful laughter.

I have been present in many services of this nature which should never have taken place. Spirit do not come to be ridiculed in such a fashion; they may have liked jokes while on earth, may have used colourful language now and again, but I have never met a spirit communicator who did not come forward with a great deal of love and respect, not just for his/her loved ones, but for the fact that s/he was allowed to be part of one of our Spiritualist Services. They draw close with dignity and often, reverence, and responding with dignity and reverence is the least we can do for them.

The joy of Spiritualist Services is that we do not sit with bowed heads, in silence; our spirit family and friends are often so funny and sometimes the mediums, while being in that altered state of awareness necessary for spirit communication to take place, often come out with some funny expressions which can bring the house down. One which springs to mind is: "Do you know a man who lost part of his leg? The bottom part!"

Laughter caused in these type of scenarios is happy laughter shared with our family and friends from both sides of life and I would never like to see it discouraged but we must clean up our act, and help make some of our Church Committees realise that 'Any medium is NOT better than no medium!" We do ourselves, and spirit a great disservice with an attitude like this.

THIS IS SPIRITUALISM

Spiritualism is the 'thinking man's religion'. As spirit awareness has slowly evolved throughout the ages, bringing in spirit communication as it did, eventually giving birth to the Science, the Religion and the Philosophy of Spiritualism, this has not changed. Spiritualism bridges faith and science to create a religion for the thinking man, for the questioning man, for the scientist, the scholar, the sceptic - in fact, for everyone. Spiritualism is not a sect and while it is happy for people to join its Churches and unfold their own spirit awareness, it does not claim to be the only religion. People are unique and all have different needs, therefore, it follows, they also have different requirements within their chosen religions and for some, the openness of Spiritualism, the lack of dogma, creed and ritual, does not sit easy with them.

Spiritualism encourages its members to investigate, to experiment, to search for truths within the framework of the religion. There are guidelines to help. Spirit teachers have been talking to mankind for many years and a lot of these teachings have been recorded, transcribed and are available within Spiritualist literature.

The most notable spirit teachings given to Spiritualism, and the world, are the 7 Principles of Spiritualism and these are:

1. The Fatherhood of God
2. The Brotherhood of Man
3. The Communion of Spirits and the Ministry of Angels
4. Continuous existence
5. Personal Responsibility
6. Compensation and Retribution for all the good and evil deeds done on earth
7. Eternal Progress open to every human soul.

Over the years Spiritualism has had to fight much ignorance and bias based on fear, usually of the unknown. Instead of people entering the Churches and seeking the truth, many decide what Spiritualism is all about, very inaccurately of course, and continue to perpetuate myths about us. The Seven Principles given by the spirit of Robert Owen and received through the trance mediumship of Emma Hardinge Britten in 1879 reflects the philosophy of Spiritualism. Unlike other religions, however, Spiritualists, when becoming Members of the Spiritualist Movement, are not required to state a belief in this Philosophy, they are asked if they accept the Seven Principles of Spiritualism, a very subtle difference.

So what form does a Spiritualist Church Service take? Really not much difference to other religions' services.

A general order of service is:

1. Welcome and Introduction
2. Opening Hymn
3. Opening Prayer and Healing Minute
4. Second Hymn
5. Inspirational Reading
6. An address by the Medium conducting the service
7. Third Hymn
8. A demonstration of mediumship by the Medium
9. Thanks and Church Notices
10. Closing Hymn
11. Closing Prayer

The address is based on Spirit Teachings or the Philosophy of Spiritualism which effectively states: 'There is no death' and in the Demonstration of Mediumship the medium will link to the world of spirit and bring forward communicators who wish to make contact with loved ones still living on earth and give evidence that they have survived death thereby giving credence to this statement.

A very simple, a very beautiful and dignified service. It is also a very happy service, often with joyful laughter resounding within the Church. I am not sure how people can fear such services, especially when many have never taken part in one. There are times when it is better to find out for yourself than listen to well-meaning friends and a Spiritualist Church Service is one of these times.

CONCLUSIONS

In conclusion, I must reiterate that apart from the obvious quotations, all the opinions expressed in this dissertation are my own. I should also like to make it quite clear that I have not used any discussion or shared experience with anyone in order to ridicule them or suggest that their views are inaccurate while mine are not.

I have looked at things which have been acknowledged as being part of Spiritualism since its inception, such as lost souls and rescue circles. I have also looked at Shapeshifters and Soul Cleansing and other such things which are starting to creep into our religion and which we must fight to stop.

I do have friends who use tarot cards, who do rescue work, who help lost souls into the light. I cannot say that I am right and they are wrong. What I do ask is that things such as these be kept out of the public arena of Spiritualism. Mediums are extremely psychic and have many abilities. They also have free will. The beauty of Spiritualism is the fact that we are allowed to think for ourselves and make our own decisions. I have rejected much on my journey through life and upon my spiritual pathway and I know that probably much of which I have discarded is perhaps very relevant; but that is my choice. I am, therefore, suggesting that we keep the private work of mediumship entirely separate from the Science, Philosophy and Religion of Spiritualism.

My dealings with spirit communicators, guides and teachers have always been spiritually elevating and I have been privileged to be the recipient of an abundance of love and joy. It distresses me, therefore, to see what is happening in Spiritualism, or more particularly, what many people are seeing as being part of Spiritualism. The silliness I have spoken about reflects upon all of us, not just the instigators of these nonsensical theories. The sadness is that people have such a need to believe in any, and/or, everything which will help take them away from some of the horrors they are having to face in life

I know of sensible people who believe they are part of a team of Ascended Masters who have incarnated to save the world; these people are practising Spiritualists!

The whole purpose of this book is to call to everyone's attention, the way in which the clear, crystal waters of Spiritualism are being polluted by so much fantastic nonsense which is slowly gathering momentum and dirtying the beautiful, natural philosophy of Spiritualism.

Our Pioneers fought long and hard in order that we might practice our religion with total freedom and they are to be applauded for their efforts. It is now time for us to face the challenges presented to Spiritualism today and fight, as they did, to preserve its truths, Spirit Teachings and all the knowledge compiled over the years and so ensure a Spiritualism of which both our Pioneers and future generations of Spiritualists can be proud.

BIBLIOGRAPHY

www.crystalhealing.org.uk
The Spirit Speaks – compiled by Tony Ortzen
Light from Silver Birch – compiled by Pam Riva
Silver Birch speaks - Edited by Sylvia Barbanell
Extemporaneous Addresses - Emma Hardinge-Britten
The Aura - Dr W J Kilner
www.spotlightministries.org.uk
www.sonic.net/~marina/
www.wikipedia.org
www.mysticfamiliar.com
www.angeltherapy.com
www.reconnections.net
www.rachelkeene.co.uk
www.marksb.info
www.Michell's Spiritual World
www.savvymoose.com
www.stressbusting.co.uk
www.vibrantuniverse.com
www.mystic-mouse.co.uk
SNU Course Notes - SD1 and SD2
www.davidicke.com
www.portalinspirations.com
www.Angelfire.com
Strangers Among Us - Ruth Montgomery

SDU PUBLICATIONS

SDU Publications prints books about mediumship and Spiritualism.

During the period we call 'Modern Spiritualism', 1848 to the current day, there have been some outstanding mediums. By keeping these books in print we preserve for future generations a record of their achievements and thereby keep their names alive.

We currently have in stock books by or about the following mediums and investigators:

- Judith Seaman
- Helen Hughes
- Nettie Colburn
- Estelle Roberts
- Emma Hardinge
- Margery Crandon
- Kathleen Goligher
- James Johnson Morse
- Daniel Dunglas Home
- Baron von Schrenck Notzing
- Vice Admiral Usborne Moore

For full details of our current catalogue:

Email:..............mail@s-upton.com
Website:..........www.s-upton.com